Michael Reisig's

Great Little Bathroom and Bedtime Book

Copyright © 2012, Clear Creek Press/Michael Reisig (reisig@ipa.net)

1st Edition, September 2012

Cover design by Powell Graphics

Cover design copyright © 2012 Clear Creek Press

Published by Clear Creek Press

P.O. Box 1081, Mena, AR 71953

1-479-394-4992

All rights reserved. No part of this publication may be reproduced, stored in a retrieval system, or transmitted in any form, or by any other means, electronic, mechanical, photocopying, recording, or otherwise, without written permission of the publisher.

ISBN: 978-0-9713694-3-6

A number of my readers have requested I add a few stories to this book that were originally published in "The Old Man's Letters," including "A Big Foot Love Story", "The Unwelcome Guest", "Facing Death Head-On", and "Spitball." Thanks to Clear Creek Press for allowing me to include these.

To my lady, Bonnie Lee, who continuously reminds me of the value of intellect and humor.

TABLE OF CONTENTS

LUCK 1
MONKEY CHATTER 4
THE CHRISTMAS STORY 7
FRIENDSHIP 10
CONTENTMENT 12
CELL PHONES 15
LOVE 18
PASSION 20
PHONE SOLICITORS AND SPACE PEOPLE 22
EVERY FORM OF REFUGE 26
RESPECT 28
A BIG FOOT LOVE STORY 31
RESPONSIBILITY 36
ADVENTURE 38
TO CHALLENGE THE HAWK 40
PIECES OF COLORED PAPER 43
THE GOOD AND THE BAD OF MODERN COMMUNICATION 45
WISDOM 48
ONE MOMENT IN TIME 50

MEMORY	52
A BEAR, A DOG, AND A SHOTGUN	55
A CHILD IS BORN	57
EQUALITY AND DEMOCRACY	59
HUMILITY	61
DIGNITY	63
CLASS AND CLASSES	65
THE UNWELCOME GUEST	67
COURAGE	71
MIRACLES	73
POWER	75
FATE, KARMA, AND DESTINY	77
LIVING AND DYING, AND 3-D GLASSES	79
WOMEN	81
HEROES…	83
COYOTES, RANCHERS, AND POINTY-HEADED PROFESSORS	86
THE GREATEST GENERATION EVER	88
TRUTH	91
FUN WITH THE PHONE SOLICITOR	93
THE AMAZING AMERICAN SOLDIER	97
TIME	99
CHICKENS	101

FAITH	104
SCHOONER AND SILO	106
IF WE COULD CLICK OUR HEELS	109
KILLING ME SOFTLY	111
IS ANYONE OUT THERE?	113
FACING DEATH HEAD ON	116
PARADISE	119
MORTALITY AND IMMORTALITY	122
SPITBALL	124
THE GOOD DEED CLAUSE	127

LUCK...

Looking back on all the adventures in my life, I realize that I have been extraordinarily lucky much of the time. I have, through the years, developed a theory – an intuition about the fundamentals of what we subscribe as luck. I call it "the baitfish theory." It's a philosophy that I have instinctively practiced since I was a young man: When out for a day's fishing, I have always taken one or two of the minnows from the bait bucket and thrown them back – set them free – because I believe that action makes me an integral part of the great Universal Infrastructure of Fortuitousness. And because I like the way it makes me feel, and that's essential also. I believe we're all really minnows in the bait bucket of life. Occasionally, given the right circumstances, the gods throw one or two of us back.

Almost all of us have encountered some traumatic, nearly impossible situation that we somehow, miraculously passed through unscathed – while some of those around us didn't. Afterwards we asked ourselves, "Why me? Why did I survive?" There are, of course, no guarantees, but I believe in order to increase your chances of being one of the surviving minnows in the traumas of life, you need to establish yourself as a card-carrying member in the Universal Infrastructure of Fortuitousness. When everything is at its bleakest point, you have to have reason to believe that the impossible is possible. Luck may be nothing more than seizing the moment with an illogical confidence.

Periodically I will go out of my way to preserve some lowly

creature that is most certainly doomed without my intervention. I stop and move turtles out of the road, or I'll catch the wasp that found his way into the house and carefully release him outside, because I like the sense of being in tune with that universal tapestry. It's a feeling of not simply living in this world, but being an innate part of the great weave, and, of course, because I understand the baitfish theory. The honest truth is, more than once in my life I have been one of the minnows the gods set free. I know what it feels like, and I am so grateful.

A week ago just at sunset, I saw that my cat had captured a huge green and gray moth with mottled, translucent wings. The cat held that poor, exquisite creature captured in its paws, pinning it against the ground. He would release it just enough to let it struggle a few inches, then pounce on it again. I couldn't help myself. I went over, grasped the cat by the scruff of the neck and gently took the moth away. It appeared battered and exhausted – probably past the point of survival. But to my surprise, as I opened my fingers the brilliant creature arched into the air, spinning upward in a dizzying spiral. His wings widened as he gathered control, and he became cool and magnificent. He headed outward toward the trees at the edge of the yard, then abruptly turned back at me, and circled my head, before dashing away. For a moment, for just an infinitesimal slick of time, I felt a wondrous revelation – a fleeting, brilliant epiphany. Suddenly I sensed the cosmos open up and I was engulfed by the spirit that binds all things together in this great weave. I suddenly, unequivocally, knew that no gift is ever forgotten in the records of life.

Who knows? Maybe the baitfish theory is just another

definition for faith – perhaps all those minnows I set free simply had more faith than their companions in the potential of divine intervention. Maybe, when they saw their opportunity, they struggled more valiantly to put themselves in my hands – who knows?

All I know for sure is they were given a chance to swim on, and so was I.

"It's hard to detect good luck – it looks so much like something you've earned." — Frank A. Clark

MONKEY CHATTER

The other day, a friend and I were talking about this journey called Life – the amazing times, the less than amazing, and the things we would change if we could simply rewind the film in a couple of places. There are moments, late at night, when all of us are challenged by the past and the future. It's a self-imposed affliction often referred to as "social anxiety," but my buddy had another name for that twilight between wake and sleep when the demons of past experiences and the challenges of the next day set upon you. He called it, "Monkey Chatter."

I laughed out loud when he told me that, because it's perfect. If you've ever spent any time in the jungle you know that there are times when the incessant cacophony of monkeys and birds can be totally distracting, or if you've ever found yourself on a major thoroughfare in New York City – same difference. Monkey Chatter affects almost everyone, but the more complex your life is, and the more you're inclined to punish yourself for past transgressions or be determined to worry about tomorrow, the more you suffer with Monkey Chatter. Sociopaths and lobotomy patients have no monkeys in their heads. The rest of us have to deal with it.

There's a line in one of my novels about a man having to make a tough choice – to risk his life rescuing his friends, or to just turn away and fly off into safety, and it epitomizes Monkey Chatter regarding the past:

"You got two choices here, Mac. You can be a hero and accumulate another genuinely outlandish tale for the next barroom, or you can stare at the ceiling fan when you lie in bed at night for the rest of your freaking life, listen to the Monkey Chatter in your head and remember what a coward you were. There are some things that wear on a man worse than death, and you're about to inherit one."

Now this is, of course, in the extreme, but it exemplifies that place which most of us understand. I came across a piece on the Internet by a writer named David Wygant, who offered this remedy for Monkey Chatter:

"Have you ever seen Nightshift? It's a really funny movie with Henry Winkler and Michael Keaton. Michael Keaton has this crazy internal voice that keeps talking, and finally, Henry Winkler says to him, "this is Chuck telling Bob to SHUT UP!"

You have to do the same thing inside your own head. "This is _____ telling Bob to SHUT UP!" Say it to yourself and start laughing about it. Calm yourself down, smile, and breathe.

You have to be able to say, so I screwed up. No big deal. You just have to ground yourself and tell yourself to shut up. It doesn't matter that you missed a beat in life. You have the abundance principle working for you – you still have the rest of your life to get it right.

As for tomorrow, here's what you need to remember – tomorrow is going to come along, bringing its challenges whether you stay up all night worrying about it or not. So tell yourself you're going to kick butt and take no prisoners in the morning, because you can do it. Tell yourself to shut up, chuckle about the name, Monkey Chatter, and go to sleep.

I'll leave with a quote by English footballer Steve Bull –

"Nerves and butterflies are fine – they're a physical sign that you're mentally ready and eager. You have to get the butterflies to fly in formation, that's the trick."

THE CHRISTMAS STORY

I thought I'd lighten the atmosphere somewhat by relating one of the funniest Christmas stories I've ever heard. It took place several years back, in Florida, and it dealt with the brother of my best friend Will.

Fred, Will's brother, always appeared to be wrapped just a little loose, as if some of the bulbs in his DNA strands were out, which might have been directly related to his excessive penchant for Wild Turkey whiskey. This particular Christmas Will bought Fred (who was a bachelor), one of those full-size blow-up dolls (complete with wig and jiggling eyeballs), as a joke. But to further the surprise, he had packaged it so that a CO_2 cartridge would activate when the ribbon on the outside of the wrapping was pulled, instantly blowing up the doll. Fred lived two houses over and would share Christmas with Will's family. In fact, it had been arranged for Fred to dress up like Santa Claus for the kids on Christmas day, so his present was left under Will's tree. In addition, packaged in a fairly secure cage under the tree was a live, six-foot python for Will's son, Mickey, who loved all sorts of reptiles and had bugged his dad for a month to get him "a really cool, big snake."

Incidentally, this story can be related with such accuracy because there was a video camera set up in the living room — to catch the kid's reactions on Christmas morning.

Well, as fate would have it, Fred, feeling a little melancholy, got really drunk Christmas eve and decided he would dress up in his Santa suit (with long white beard) and deliver his presents to his brother's family in traditional fashion. It was well after midnight and everyone was sound asleep when Fred, with a bag of presents slung over his shoulder, jimmied the lock on the patio door and snuck/stumbled into Will's living room. In the dimness, illuminated only by a handful of Christmas tree ornaments, Fred lurched over and began dragging out presents and putting them around the tree, humming a demented version of "Deck the Halls." In the process, he noticed a present with his name on it. Pulling out his pint of Wild Turkey, he took a solid swig and picked up his present. He shook it, without satisfaction. Heck, no one would know if he just took a quick peek inside.

He grabbed the ribbon and pulled it.

The package exploded like a Claymore mine as the giant doll with jiggling eyeballs and outstretched arms inflated with a high, compressed-air scream and came bursting out of the box like a scene from The Mummy's Revenge. Fred shrieked like a teenage girl as the doll's arms caught in his beard hair and he stumbled backwards, fighting off what he was certain (in his snockered state) was some underworld demon. As he fell rear-first into the embers of the fireplace, the doll locked to him in loving embrace, the fur around the waistline of his jacket caught fire. Still wailing like a banshee, Fred lurched up, grabbed a fireplace poker, and, staggering around the room in smoke and flames, began frantically stabbing his assailant. The doll's eyes finally rolled back and it gave up with a sigh of air, collapsing on Fred, who ripped it off of him and threw it on the floor, then tore off his jacket and started stomping on both of them alternately while screaming obscenities.

Collapsing into a chair as most of Will's terrified family

reached the landing of the stairs, Fred had just begun to feel he had survived the ordeal, when he suddenly felt something slither up his right pants leg. Still fairly drunk, it took him a moment to assess the situation, but when "Monty" the python (who had managed to wedge open the cage door and slither to freedom) pushed his head out of Fred's waistband and slurped out a long, forked tongue in greeting, Christmas was over for Santa.

Fred's entire body stiffened like he'd just mainlined a quart of curare and his mouth started to move, making tiny incoherent sounds. But when Monty slithered upwards onto his chest, Santa really lost it. Grabbing the snake by the neck and making screechy, yipping noises like a Chihuahua that's been stepped on, Fred once again lurched to his feet and began a second demented dance around the living room. This was all the family terrier could stand and he joined the fray on the side of the snake, grabbing Santa solidly by the rear. Careening across the living room, snake solidly clutched at arm's length, dog dangling tenaciously from his buttocks, screeching expletives, stomping on presents and taking half the Christmas tree decorations with him, Fred stumbled through the patio screen door and into the pool on the other side.

When he had recovered from the fright, the burns and the hangover, uncle Fred apologized to everyone. They all forgave him easily – he had started out with good intentions and had given them an outstanding present – a Christmas film clip that made the best of "America's Funniest Videos" look like a church service.

FRIENDSHIP

It's been an interesting trip, this life. I'm old enough now, to look back at the hills and valleys of my journey with a degree of introspection. As you get on in years you're more able to discern what is really valuable in this short quest. To those young people out there just starting this sojourn, one of the messages I would scribble down and thrust into their pockets as they pass, is to take the time to nurture friendships along the way — and how valuable true friendships become as we grow older.

We inevitably gather people to us as we walk through life. Most brush against us for a while and pass on, perhaps becoming memories that prompt an occasional smile — vague faces, and names on the tips of our tongues. But every once in a while someone comes into our lives and the ease of their presence is not so much like meeting a new friend but encountering an old one again. (You understand, don't you? And a name comes to mind immediately). Sometimes this happens when we've aged enough to identify it, but often it happens in the impetuousness and confusion of youth, and for the careless, the jewel can slip between our fingers then, because real friendship requires attentiveness for it to become enduring — it is a slow-ripening fruit. And like fine wines, the old friendships often become the best.

Friends, true friends, offer a priceless gift — memories. Like the photographs in a tattered album, you can take out these memories and page through them at any time. A simple phone call and a brief walk down an old, well-remembered road can have a remarkable effect on the complexion of the day.

Scribbled on that note to young folks I would add in bold letters, that every form of refuge has its price, and the payment here requires continuous effort — accepting the trauma and the triumph of another's life with equal earnestness. Some of us turn to spirit, some of us to poetry, but most of us need a friend in the valleys of our lives. So go out there and ferret out that acorn of true friendship. Nurture it, let it curl around the times of your life, unfolding through the years into a solid oak that you can lean against in the hard times, draw comfort from the depth of its roots, and pause in its shelter along this journey.

To the dear friends who have shared my triumphs and tragedies I would say, once again, thank you, for I have leaned on you more than once, and now, after all these years, it is a wondrous and secure feeling to know that in this vast forest of deciduous relationships and seasonal alliances, there is still a tree or two that would shelter me.

"Think where man's glory most begins and ends, and say my glory was, I had such friends..." — *William Butler Yeats*

CONTENTMENT...

"The poor seek riches, the rich seek heaven, but the wise seek tranquility..."

I've always liked that expression, but I think it misses the mark a little. The part that the above equation omits is, contentment, for almost everything pales without contentment.

Having spent nearly half a dozen decades on this ball of dirt and water I've come to realize a few things. First off, wealth isn't the end-all-to-beat-all, but I will say this – the person who said money can't buy happiness didn't have money. It is certain that riches can buy some peace of mind, but they won't buy integrity, compassion, or real friendship – those things are strictly earned – and money, by and large, doesn't buy contentment. I've been fairly rich and I've been dirt poor in this life, and what I've discovered about money is that it's most conspicuous in its absence.

This mercurial commodity, contentment, is the sister of happiness – but you can be dizzily happy and still not be content. Just ask the guy (or girl) who plays the blackjack or roulette table. I've seen people ecstatic over the windfall a lucky roll has given them (a year's wages or more), but were they content? If they had been, they wouldn't have lost it all before the night was over.

Heaven, of course, is something most all of us want. I've discovered its value becomes more conspicuous with age. Heaven isn't high on a teenager's list of priorities – but ask someone in their late 70s.

The thing about heaven is, nearly every religious philosophy in the world has a different view of it – I figure there's bound to be a heck of a lot of surprised people popping up on the other side. In my opinion, many of the orthodox views of heaven I've heard aren't least bit appealing – I don't like harp music, the idea of wings could be just purely annoying when you're trying to sit down or sleep, and continuously singing spiritual hymns would just make me crazy. I've given it some thought, and I may be better off in hell, because that's probably where most of my friends will be – sweating off their evil ways and listening to Santana and Jimmy Buffett. Ultimately, contentment is about finding that niche in life (or maybe death) where you fit.

Tranquility is nice, I guess, but when I consider the term tranquility, the thing that always comes to mind is sort of a navel-contemplating Prozac latitude – that "one herb brownie too many" insightfulness where you're just amazed with the texture of the stucco on the walls.

Don't get me wrong. I like the idea of being tranquil, but I don't think being tranquil translates one hundred percent into being content.

I guess the truth is, really tranquil people annoy me. I like being a little on edge. I like people knowing that if you push me too far I might punch you out. I'm content with knowing I might do that.

So, I guess what this all comes down to is, contentment is a work in progress. It is as much about liking yourself as it is having others like you. It's about having enough money to put a down payment on happiness, but recognizing that you have to keep paying into that nest egg with a commitment of integrity and effort to make it work. It's about accepting the anxieties of life with a degree of serenity, but standing up for what you believe in at the same time, and it's feeling good about the future – carrying a certainty in your breast that wonderful things are still possible, and that even the end of this life is nothing more than the beginning of another extraordinary experience.

I'll leave you with one of my favorite quotes by the Greek philosopher Epicurus:

"Do not spoil what you have by desiring what you have not; remember that what you now have was once among the things you only hoped for."

CELL PHONES

For the life of me, I don't quite understand this addiction to cell phones that has manifested itself in our society. I understand their utilitarian value – being able to contact authorities in an emergency or get in touch with the wife to let her know you'll be late getting home, but lately, everywhere I look, someone's got a cell phone umbilically attached to their ear, oblivious to the rest of the world. This seems exceptionally prevalent while driving, and this makes life more challenging for all of us.

Let's face it, doing things other than driving while driving is almost a national pastime – smoking, drinking, eating, reprimanding children, playing with pets, putting on makeup, and now we have talking on the phone (while doing all the aforementioned things as well). I've seen Chinese circus acts that couldn't hold a candle to the everyday drivers on our local highway, but it's not just on the road. How many times have you been waiting at the doctor's office or an airport concourse, or having lunch at a nice restaurant, when someone sits down close to you, drags out a cell phone and begins a conversation that is just loud enough to be really annoying. I don't want to know a whole bunch of intimate things about you, your boyfriend or your family. I don't want to know how important you are.

I had to go to Little Rock the other day. In the process, I had to make a pit stop at a rest area. I walked into the less than stellar bathroom, a little cautious to begin with. The first stall was taken so I tried the second. It opened – seat still attached to the commode, water in the toilet not terribly brown, toilet paper available — all good signs. I had just sat down when I hear a voice from the next stall...

"Hi there, how is it going?"

All right, I'm not generally inclined to strike up conversations with strangers in washrooms on the side of the road, but the voice continues.

"Can you hear me okay?"

I didn't know exactly what to do, so finally I said, "Yeah, I hear you. I'm okay..."

Then the voice says, "So, what are you doing?"

Now, I find that a bit disconcerting, and just a little put out, I say, "Well, I'm headed to Little Rock, and right now I'm taking a crap!"

Then I hear the person say, all flustered, "Look, I'll call you back, every time I ask you a question some idiot in the stall next to me keeps answering."

If you're not sure whether you're addicted to your cell phone, here's a short battery of questions I found on the web to help you out.

1. Do parts of your body tingle when you get free cell phone minutes?

2. Does raising your children interfere with programming your speed dial?

3. Do you have long-distance conversations while sitting on the toilet in public restrooms?

4. Does the term, "fashion statement" mean matching your

outfit with your cell phone carrying case?

5. Do you use the menu light as your nightlight?

I hate to sound chauvinistic, but I think young girls and cell phones are absolutely the worst combination. I was driving to work this morning, and as I looked over to my left, there was a young woman in a Honda doing 50 miles an hour in a 35 mph zone, with her face tilted up to her rear view mirror, putting on her eyeliner while ardently talking on a cell phone. The next thing I knew, she was halfway into my lane.

It scared me so badly I dropped my electric shaver into my latte.

LOVE

I don't have to tell you that there's something absolutely magical about the divine intervention of love. Ordinary people become princes and princesses, all the sunsets are created by Monet, the wind smells richer, and the very placement of the stars seem designed for your pleasure. But in the process, you discover that much of the joy in life becomes frighteningly conditional — built around a single soul and their continued contentment with you.

Each of us loves a little differently, and sometimes you have to accept that just because a person doesn't love you in the fashion you've envisioned, doesn't mean they're not providing you with all the love they have. You have to be wise enough to determine if what they're offering will be sufficient to feed your head and your heart. (And you generally have to make the decision while still in the midst of this temporary insanity — which makes it nothing short of a roll of the dice.)

Love... You're sucked into the vortex of this delightful torment with another soul, but the two images of love you share must blend enough to become a sufficiently pliable amalgam that whirls in concert with the vortex, gradually slowing and cooling from white hot to a temperature and a mass that's comfortable for the two of you. It's the transformation from being wildly in love to loving. It's the process that provides longevity to affection. If this doesn't happen, one of you (or both of you), will be forced out the small end of the swirling tunnel, generally with a good deal of kicking and screaming.

There is, of course the alternate possibility that at some point in the cooling process your vision will clear and you'll realize you've aligned yourself with an insufferable boor or an unmitigated asshole. At which point you generally just push said boor or asshole out the small hole.

Love is a brilliant, colorful, carnival ride that leaves you with the lights of the midway and the smell of cotton candy for the rest of your life. Never let the anticipation of disappointment overshadow the expectation of sheer thrill. Take a chance. Step into that precariously swaying bench and tell the carnie at the lever to throw it into high gear, because love may not be what makes the Ferris wheel spin, but it's what makes the ride memorable.

I'll leave you with one of my favorite expressions:

Love is a lot like contracting rabies. Sometime after you've been bitten you know you're getting crazy, but there's nothing you can do about it.

PASSION...

Intelligence is powerful, will is a motivator, love is a carnival of delightful emotions, but passion is the cornerstone of our lives. It defines who we are and what we will become. It's the centerpiece in all our accomplishments, the rod that stokes the fire in all our endeavors. It drives love to its highest peaks. It's the essence of great art, intellectual advancement, and extraordinary athletic prowess. When we are fortunate enough to find commitment, exuberance, and pleasure in one place, then we have fallen victim to passion.

But passion can be a two-edged sword. It can be as tragic as any Shakespearean play or perhaps more aptly put, it is the tragedy in the Shakespeare play – the lover gone mad with grief, the myopic mate, the gambler's obsession. As with all things, we must hold tightly the reins of our passions and temper them with reason, lest they run away with us.

There are those who drink from the goblet of passion continuously and there are those who have never tasted it, and neither understands the other. I'm reminded of the quote by Angela Monet; "Those who danced were thought to be quite mad by those who could not hear the music." To carry passion in your breast is to never cease to grow, because you are always finding something new with which to be enthralled.

To me, passion is the seasoning of life. Most of us are given a plate at birth with much the same entrees as others – the endless possibilities for success, love, learning, compassion, etc. It's whether you flavor those entrees with passion and give them as much tang as you can that makes the difference. You can only hope to be one of the dancers who hear the music.

How often, when reading about the great accomplishers of our times, have you learned about their extraordinary commitment? From George Washington and Martin Luther King, to Bill Gates and Vince Lombardi, passion is the father of ambition, desire, and energy. Never underestimate it, in yourself or others. One of the greatest gifts parents can give their children is passion – the enthusiasm for honesty, love, kindness, and commitment. Your passion not only changes you, it changes the world around you. Every great dream begins with a spark. It's the passion within us that turns it to flame – or the lack of passion that allows it to die.

Ask yourself today; what are my passions? Am I exercising my passions – living them, allowing them to make my life and the lives of those around me better? Can I hear the music, or am I just watching others dance...

"Without passion, man is a mere latent force and possibility, like the flint that awaits the shock of iron before it can give forth its spark." — Henri-Frederic Amiel, 1856

PHONE SOLICITORS AND SPACE PEOPLE

Just lately it seems that a whole new gaggle of phone solicitors have found my home phone number. I can think of little that irritates me more than having the few hours of relaxation I get in the evenings interrupted by a phone jackal. Last Sunday night – of all nights, I was ripped from my reverie twice by two idiots, one from a mortgage company and one offering time-share apartments.

At that point I decided to revert to my cunning, devious self – it was payback time. The following morning I went out and purchased a few items – an air horn, some blanks for my .22 pistol, and the CD, War of the Worlds.

The next evening I ran the CD forward to the spot I was looking for, laid my pistol and the air horn by the phone, brought the dogs in from outside and leashed them to the table next to the phone, then got a BBQ rib from last night's dinner and set it on the table. Then I set back and waited.

Fortunately it wasn't a long wait. The phone rang. I picked it up.

"Hello?"

"Hello? Is this Michael Reesiig?" (Bad pronunciation of my name – I knew I had one.)

"Yes, this is he," I replied.

"Well, good evening Michael. My name is Wilbie Landstrom from United Federal Mortgage and Life Insurance. Do you have a life insurance policy Michael?"

I hate it when people I don't know overuse my first name – but I smiled to myself.

"Well, I have some insurance but I don't know if I have enough…" I replied.

I could hear the suppressed glee in Wilbie's voice. "Well you can never have enough life insurance – you have to consider your loved ones. Michael, I can offer you –"

"Sorry to interrupt Weenie… but the train is coming. I live near a railroad track."

"No, my name is Wilbie"

"Wilbie, huh?" I said with an edge of distain. "That's not much better than Weenie. Hold just a moment – here comes the train."

At that point I put the air horn to the phone and let off a five-second burst. I'm pretty sure I heard Weenie scream.

I quickly put the phone to my ear again: "Hello Willie, are you still there?"

"It's Wilbie," said the shaken voice at the other end.

"Okay, okay, so how much is this insurance gonna cost me and what does it cover?

Weenie gathered himself together and tried again. "We can offer several policies to fit your needs, and if you buy a policy tonight we will offer you two free days at our timeshare in –"

"Hold on Willie that damn train is backing up again."

I squeezed off another blast of the air horn. That time I was certain I heard him scream.

"Look, Willie, I'm really sorry. The train's gone now – won't be another for a half-hour."

"Wilbie…"

"Okay, So, tell me, how is my age going to affect my policy price?"

"Not really very much, we can put you into a graduating scale of –"

At that point I picked up the BBQ rib and held it above the dogs, who immediately started barking. "Sorry Willie, but there's something going on outside. I live way out in the country – gotta check…"

I put the phone on the table backed away and picked up the bone again. The dogs responded with another chorus and in the background I shouted "My Lord! I don't believe it. It's a freaking spaceship hovering over the top of the house! Heaven help us all! My God! Look at them creatures! Get the gun, Ma! It's aliens! We're being abducted!"

At that point I hit the button on the War Of The Worlds CD and the scene where the alien ships are humming and shooting up the city. I picked up my pistol, moved to the door and fired a few rounds into the air. (Bang! Bang! Bang!) (Pause) "Oh sweet Jesus!" (Bang! Bang! Bang!)

I moved over closer to the phone and screamed, "They got Ma! Shoot Ma! Shoot! Don't let 'em take you! (Bang! Bang!). "Dear God! I accidently shot Ma!" I quickly moved back and grabbed the phone. "Willie! Willie! For God's sake call the government. Good Lord! They're eatin' the dogs (bone held high – more whining and barking.) "Run for your life Willie!" I screamed into the phone. "They gonna kill us *aaaalllll!"* Then I hit the disconnect lever on the phone cradle.

I waited for a couple minutes, got Wilbie's number from the caller ID and dialed it. Sure enough, a fairly shaken, familiar voice answered meekly, *"Yeess..."*

In a deep, menacingly rasping tone I growled out, *"WHHOOO ARREE YOOUUU?? WHEEREE ARREE YOOUUU?? WHOO ARREE YOOUUU...."* I could hear Wilbe in the background making little yippy sounds from the back of his throat, like a Chihuahua strangling on a chewstick, then he just burbled up into a full-fledged shriek and the phone went dead.

Now, every once in a while in the evenings when I'm a little bored, I'll pick up the phone, block out my number and call Weenie. When he picks up I say, *"WHHOOO ARREE YOOUUU? WHEEREE ARREE YOOUUU?"* Then I hang up.

EVERY FORM OF REFUGE...

I was speaking with an acquaintance the other day, about the places we choose to spend our lives, and why. I was reminded of an expression in a song by Don Henley and the Eagles – "Every form of refuge has its price." It became one of my favorite sayings, and throughout my life, through all my travels – the places I've stayed and the places that have stayed with me – I have come to realize how true those words were.

There's no such thing, really, as the perfect refuge. Still, we are all free to search for the location that captures most of our heart and gives the majority of amenities that provide us peace of mind, then we must accept the good we've found with the inevitable less than good.

In this life, so many people simply lock themselves to a spot like an oyster to a rock, never looking over the horizon – accepting, refusing to dream. A few are content, but most are just fearful of vision and chance. Some of us are searchers, and we need more. We want a land that warms the heart – that strikes such a note at the core of our being that we stand there enthralled, soothed, and a voice inside says, "I'm home." We want to choose the point for our joys and sorrows before we experience them.

But here's the truth about oysters and seekers – no matter where you go, you have to take yourself with you, and much of the happiness that is derived for a person anywhere they end up is direct result of how content they are with the soul staring back in the mirror.

When you look toward the horizon and consider packing up, you have to envision yourself as an old jacket or a weathered dress – time has changed the garment but is it still your favorite? Does it still feel warm and good when you put it on, and most of all, would you take it with you?

I believe it's okay to be a searcher – go find that land and sky that satisfies and fulfills, but never lose sight of the importance of the baggage you carry, and remember that ultimately, growth comes more from directing the voyage and weathering the storms than from proclaiming a destination.

We all occasionally take a moment of introspection and reminiscence on the far side of this voyage. Amongst the faded shirts and worn shoes of my baggage, I sometimes, quite by accident, discover a memory hidden within the folds of another time. I hold it for a moment and it warms me, like a small, precious gift from an old friend. It lightens my load on the final few miles of this journey – and I am grateful.

RESPECT...

Respect — a commodity that is required by some, commanded by others, and desired by all. There are three kinds of respect — that of yourself, that of others, and a broad respect for life, living things, and the world we live in, which may well be the most elemental and defining of a person. We all want people to respect us, and we're bitter if, for some reason they don't. But we all know that in our quiet hours we are often our own greatest critics, because no one remembers our failures and our shortcomings as well as we do.

Without respect for yourself you can never establish discipline, or maintain a valued set of morals, or possess dignity. Respect for one's self is what feeds character and denies you the ability to lie, cheat, or steal with any sense of comfort. Respect for others is the nexus of friendship, it is the mortar that bonds everything from platoons and corporations, to religions. Being "liked" pales to being "respected." Being liked is one-dimensional, being respected comes with multi-dimensional value.

Respect is not only significant in individual relationships, it is imperative in a society's relationship with its government. It may seem contradictory, but a people's willingness to obey the law is commensurate with the number of regulations a government feels required to thrust upon them. The more legislations, the more regulations a government creates, the less people feel a moral obligation to abide by them. Overregulation epitomizes a government's lack of trust and respect for its citizenry, and we are the most legislated nation in the world.

Respect is never free, it always comes with a price, yet we live in a society that has begun to market respect as if it were a commodity, and demand it as if it were a birthright. Money can buy you power, but it's knowledge and character that are the currencies of respect. Luck never buys respect, no matter how much you possess. In fact, blatant, unfettered luck is often viewed with an envy that can bleed into distain. Ask any major lottery winner.

The bond that ties you to family, friends, and ultimately to those with whom you chose to spend your life is not love, but respect. Love inevitably fades from white-hot to a tempered warmth, but the flame that feeds any relationship throughout, is respect. That is the cornerstone of virtue and the foundation of all relationships. It is the key to determining a person's character, and it applies in numerous fashions throughout life:

* A future wife should watch how a man respects his mother. It will tell her what she can expect.

* Never trust anyone who is cruel to animals. If they have no respect for lesser creatures, they lack the true essence of compassion.

* A man who constantly interrupts others while they are speaking has no respect for them.

* A person who lies to anyone in your presence will lie to you.

* The purest form of respect is always mutual. Remember that you're never required to be the designated driver for someone else's intoxicated ego.

I'll leave you with a quote from American author Joan Didion:

"The willingness to accept responsibility for one's own life is the source from which self-respect springs."

A BIG FOOT LOVE STORY

I was talking with a friend the other day about the concept of "Big Foot" or "Sasquatch," and apparently some alleged sightings in our area of this controversial creature. It reminded me of the story about that buddy of mine who once bought a gorilla suit and a Tina Turner wig and used to scare late-night motorists on a road near his house. It's a little long, but I thought I'd pass it on, for those of you who might need a chuckle...

Burt was just naturally wrapped a little loose. He watched a documentary on the Big Foot phenomenon one night and became so intrigued, he chased down every scrap of information he could find on the creatures. Then he began scouring the hills in Arkansas for signs of a Sasquatch. When, eventually he couldn't find one, he simply decided to become one.

Usually, after about half a bottle of Old Jack, Burt would throw his gorilla suit and his wig in the pickup and drive to a lonely area where the road entered the National Forest. He'd park the truck out of sight, don his costume and wait in the woods by the road for an approaching set of headlights. When the unsuspecting motorist got fairly close, Burt would lumber out into the middle of the highway and raise his arms menacingly at the lights, then he'd high-tail it into the woods on the other side laughing like a hyena. He did this for quite some time and had begun to enjoy the reports of Big Foot sightings that were circulating throughout the area, but all the fun came to an abrupt end one night for old Burt. He swears this story is true. Personally, I'm not sure how much the whisky had to do with it, but this is the tale anyway...

One night, Burt had planted himself and his bottle of "Old Jack" in the woods and had already raised the blood pressure of several motorists, when he saw the lights of a big pickup headed his way. Little did he know that seated in that truck were a couple of guys who were nearly as Neanderthal as the creature he was imitating.

Frank Flip and his brother Vernon were just returning from an unsuccessful evening of poaching deer in the National Forest. They'd been sharing a jug of moonshine since about 10 p.m., and both were three sheets to the wind. When old Burt came out of the woods, he was pretty well lit himself. He crabbed his way out to the center of the road and raised his hands, pausing a little longer than normal – his liquor-fuddled mind not quite registering how close the approaching truck was. About the time he decided to get on the move, he stumbled, sprawling out on the shoulder of the road like a truck-struck raccoon. Frank and Vernon were way too drunk (and probably too stupid) to be afraid of the giant hairy creature in the road. The pickup screeched to a halt and the Flip brothers stumbled out, guns in hand – they hadn't bagged a deer that night, but a Big Foot mounted on the wall would be even better.

Burt scrambled to his feet with the sound of gunshots in the air and turf exploding around him. With a high-pitched scream, he was off and running, undoubtedly setting a Guinness World Book of Records for the fastest 100-yard dash by an imitation Sasquatch. He made it to the woods as bullets thudded into trees around him, his ears filled with the slurred shouts of the Flip brothers, still very much bent on having them a Big Foot. Burt headed straight into the woods—the Flips close behind. They probably would have caught him, but Vernon, in his unbridled enthusiasm, ran smack-dab into the low hanging limb of a pine tree, knocking himself out. By the time Frank brought him around, Burt was well gone and headed for the deep woods.

Old Burt ran until his heart sounded like a blacksmith's hammer and his breath was coming in locomotive gasps. Finally, he just flat wore out and collapsed to the ground. Burt said he stayed like that for about 10 minutes—just lying there, trying to catch his breath. It was as still as a graveyard, the only sounds were the ragged breaths he drew. A sliver of a moon had risen above the trees, casting an eerie glow through the boughs and onto the forest floor. Burt was about to get up when he heard a sound, like a branch being moved... Then he heard another sound. Something was moving in the periphery of the darkness around him. Something big. He could hear the dry leaves crackling underfoot with each slow deliberate step. At first he thought it might be one of the crazies who had tried to shoot him, but he had lost them way back. Besides, something in the back of his mind told him that wasn't it. There was a smell in the air — the heavy, musty blend of an animal's lair — of matted hair and feces, and old earth. Burt had just decided that this was no longer a good place to be and began to rise, when there was a guttural grunt from the darkness, and something reached around him from behind and jerked him to his feet — something with huge hairy arms, something that smelled like a badly maintained badger cage.

Now you have to bear in mind here that Burt was still dressed as a Sasquatch —complete with gorilla suit and Tina Turner wig. With a quick shift of his shoulders, he managed to twist around just enough to get a glance at his captor's face. It was a vision right out of the X-Files – huge yellow teeth, flared nostrils and a pair of deep-set, haunted eyes that carried the strangest glint... That was enough for our gorilla boy. He fainted dead away.

When Burt came to seconds later, he felt something licking the back of his neck. The creature still held him tightly – but not painfully – as it licked the neck of Burt's gorilla suit and issued a throaty moan. At that point, Burt said he was aware of two things – one: the creature was a male, and two: it really liked him. Well, being a love toy for an eight-foot Big Foot was right up there with the top 10 things Burt never wanted to have happen to him – right next to leprosy, root canals, and hemorrhoid surgery. Burt said he was beginning to feel like he was starring in a new version of Deliverance directed by Stephen King. A final insistent shove from Mr. Big Foot was all the prompting old Burt needed. Fight or flight adrenaline hit his system in a rush and flight definitely won out. Burt threw his arms up and broke the grip of his lusty new friend and was gone like Black Beauty on bennies, leaving Big Foot with nothing but a wig in his hand and an ache in his... heart. As he streaked into the darkness of the woods, Burt said he was fairly certain he broke his first world record for the 100-yard dash. As he tore through the underbrush, he could hear the mournful wails of his hairy companion growing fainter in the distance.

Well, Burt ran until he was purely exhausted again, but as luck would have it, he had run in the right direction and had come out on the road. That was the good news. The bad news was he'd emerged less than 75 yards from the Flip brothers, who were just getting into their truck to leave. Frank spotted "the goll-derned Big Foot" and the race was on again. As the

Flips came pouring out of the pickup, guns blazing, Burt started screaming incoherently about not being a frigging Big Foot and ripped the gorilla head off to show them. That would have worked, if he had been dealing with rational people. Vernon took one look at Burt and shouted, "He pulled his goll-derned head off! Shoot the heeaaad! Shoot the heeaaad! When a 30.06 round slapped the front of the head, jerking it out of Burt's hand, he realized negotiation was not going to be an issue. In a blink he was headed back into the woods, unzipping and ripping off the gorilla suit as he stumbled along at breakneck speed (probably another Guinness Book record).

About an hour later, a state highway patrol officer was cruising along when he spotted Burt in nothing but his underwear, waving at him from the side of the road. Later, the officer was heard to remark that normally when they came across someone naked on the highway, they had to chase them down. This particular guy not only wanted to be caught and taken to the police station, he wanted to be locked in the trunk on the way there.

Needless to say, Burt gave up his late night escapades. The Flip brothers never got a Sasquatch to mount on the wall, and if this story's true, somewhere out in those woods is a lovelorn Big Foot with nothing but a Tina Turner wig and the memory of what might have been...

Yes, love can be such a fleeting thing – or is that fleeing?

RESPONSIBILITY

I grew up in a responsible world – on a personal and family level, and a national level. You had responsibilities, you were required to perform, to accomplish, and your character was borne from those accomplishments and performances. Your parents and your school, and even your community expected you to live up to standards, and if you didn't you were the exception, not the norm.

We hadn't discovered the power of the excuse yet, or entitlement. We hadn't yet encountered the converse strength in being a "victim." You were entitled to what you worked for – nothing more, nothing less.

Things have changed – in less than one lifetime.

Most importantly, back then these new concepts of entitlement and victimization hadn't bled into government. Today we debate our rights, demand privileges, and expect entitlements, instead of accepting the fact that with liberty comes responsibility. If you want no responsibility then you have to sacrifice self-respect and at that point you have no right to demand anything. If you insist that the government takes care of you, then you forfeit the right to question what it does – responsibility is the price of freedom. When you constantly wait for someone else to make your life richer and fuller you have suspended your own will, and I have always thought it is the ultimate folly to accept that your prosperity is being taken care of for you.

I am amazed by how many excuses people can come up with

for their failures. You are not responsible for your childhood experiences and the programming that came with them. You are however, responsible for fixing it as an adult. Until you accept the fact that you are morally responsible for your actions you will always be a victim of circumstance, and you can dodge your responsibilities, but you can't dodge the consequences of those actions.

Ultimately the concept of good government is to make its citizens responsible, for the more responsible a society, the less government it needs. The sister of responsibility is obligation, and obligation is not always about huge sacrifice but more often about habitual compassion and character. We need to become people who say, "I must do something," not "something must be done."

You are the driver of the vehicle that is your life – you are not a passenger. Where you go is entirely up to you. When you arrive at various destinations, don't blame anyone else for misreading the map. Responsibility seems to have become a transferable burden easily placed at the feet of fate, gods, or insufficient luck, when in reality that burden has never belonged to anyone else but you. I would love to see a class in responsibility become standard curriculum in all schools. Then perhaps our children's children would be left with something other than chaos.

I'll leave you with a quote from Dr. Jonas Salk:

"Our greatest responsibility is to become good ancestors."

ADVENTURE

Not everyone appreciates adventure, because it oftentimes comes with a price, but for many of us it's simply an essential part of who we are, and the risk is what makes the experience sweet.

Actually, adventure is the raw unearthing of experience when you're least prepared for it, and genuine adventures are usually appreciated more in retrospect. It's why they made alcohol — for the recounting of adventures. When that first primitive man told the story of how he brought down the charging bison single-handedly, they nodded and grunted with respect around the fire. But a few years later, when they'd figured out how to distil daffodil pedals, that same story had them shouting and dancing in the firelight with their spears, jabbing the darkness around them with vigor and courage and slapping their companion on the back.

The truth is, the adventure for which you can buy a ticket, or purchase a week in advance, generally doesn't have any red meat on the plate. Real adventure isn't available mail-order, it isn't delivered to the door like pizza. You have to actively seek the extraordinary, and make preparations for its happening — then what you discover is, much of the actual sequence is totally spontaneous and often initiated with an expletive or two.

The byproduct of the whole adventure thing is knowledge (and, of course, wonderful barroom stories). Great experiences are borne not from what happens to you, but from how you respond when they're happening. If you're paying attention, encapsulated in the event is learning – which enables you to limit your next battery of mistakes to something new. The man who picks up a cat by the tail is about to have a learning experience – not necessarily an adventure.

Almost everyone has a golden recollection in their past – from which they draw to refuel life in the present. Very often, those memories are the product of some stretch of their imagination, a few moments in their life where they chose to believe in the impossible.

Many of us have molded our imaginations to fit impossible situations. The result was remarkable experiences that became memorable adventures. And we've shared the distinct pleasure of dancing around the fire with friends and jabbing our spears at the darkness many a time.

I'm going to close now, but I'll leave you with line or two from a book I'm sure you'll recognize:

"I can't believe in impossible things," said Alice.

"I daresay you haven't had much practice," said the Queen. "When I was your age, I always did it for half-an-hour a day. Why, sometimes I believed in as many as six impossible things before breakfast."

TO CHALLENGE THE HAWK

As I was driving to work the other day, I watched a small flock of Starlings chasing a large Red-Tailed Hawk across the sky. The group of birds, each individually insignificant and helpless against the hawk, had banded together and were routing the more powerful bird in swift, concerted attacks. It was not the act itself that I found so remarkable, but the choreography of evolution that made it possible.

As I watched the hawk weave its way through the sky in harassed retreat, I was certain that the victory I was witnessing had been purchased with the lives of countless Starlings over hundreds of generations in a process of courage, cognizance, and gradual understanding.

At some time, perhaps thousands of years ago, when the hawk still reigned unchecked over flocks of Starlings and their fledglings, one bird chose one day to make a stand. I could imagine the hawk descending with cold confidence on a mating grounds or a hatchery of Starlings. His presence was answered with startled warning cries and the rush of wings as the birds broke from the flock, swirling and darting away in panicked abandon – all but one that is.

He (or most probably, she) in angry defiance perhaps born of that most powerful of emotions, maternal instinct, turned and threw herself up at him. The hawk was taken by surprise and veered for just a moment, before turning sharply, locking on the bird and killing it in a shock wave of momentum.

Perhaps that single act of defiance wasn't even noticed – or *maybe it was* — and the fact that the hawk had veered, however briefly, was buried in the back of the mind of every Starling that witnessed it.

Somewhere along the line — a day, a month, or even a year later — another bird arched away from the flock and challenged the hawk in a brilliant moment of courage and sacrifice. It died like the first. But others had watched the hawk flinch again, just for a second. It could be that scores of individual Starlings followed that example of resolution and bravery for years afterwards. Some, with their short wings and infinitely tighter flight patterns than the bigger bird, actually survived the ordeal, and the flock watched, and remembered.

Perhaps offering up one's self for the safety of the flock became the thing to do with the younger birds — a rite of passage, a testimony of mettle and spirit — who knows? Still, most died, until one day, two Starlings rose from the flock and attacked the hawk together. Taken by surprise, the hawk was confused and missed both birds on the first pass, and the rest of the flock got away.

Who knows how long it was before a third and a fourth Starling charged the hawk, or when it was that the first Starling twisted sharply in the sky and fell on the big bird from behind, striking the initial blow for an entire genus. The only thing I'm certain of is that it happened, and at that moment, the lives of Starlings and hawks changed forever.

I'm writing this on Veteran's Day, on a bench not far from the courthouse, in a small square where the monument to our fallen soldiers rests. As the morning sun brushes that burnished stone, highlighting familiar names and distant *places, I'm reminded that few things of importance in this world are accomplished without courage. And nowhere in our society is courage more epitomized than in our Armed Forces. The men and women of America's military are the ones who have always been willing to make the necessary sacrifice — for the flock. They are the mettle and the spirit of this country, and on this day I feel small and humbled as I read those names etched in stone — the names of those who challenged the hawk, for the rest of us.*

PIECES OF COLORED PAPER

"Money is the barometer of a society's virtue." – Ayn Rand

Watching the news last night I was reminded of what a profound influence money has on all that takes place on this spinning ball of dirt and water. It appears, without a doubt, that the great motivator for this planet is small, colored strips of paper imprinted with pictures of mostly dead leaders.

We all toil fervently at our various tasks, anxious with anticipation for nothing more than colored strips of paper distributed by our government. We have great structures dedicated to the storage of these strips. Some of us occasionally invade these structures in an attempt to steal these strips. We often kill each other over these colored strips. Entire governments and cultural systems can collapse if they run out of these little pieces of colored paper.

Every once in a while some enterprising individual decides to make their own strips of paper, which causes considerable furor with the folks who claim that privilege. Oddly enough everyone else is quite comfortable with the homemade strips, until they're told they weren't made by the right people.

We carry little books containing pages with blank lines in them (that are magically conjoined to strips of paper), and we simply write in arbitrary amounts on those pages, tear them out, and people give us things for the paper. Amazing, isn't it?

There is great respect given to those who have the most

strips of paper, but here's another lingering irony; much of the time the accumulation of those pieces of colored paper have actually made that person less respectable.

We are fraught with religions on this planet, yet the thing we all seem to worship most is strips of paper. In fact, in one of the greatest ironies, the leaders of many religious congregations preach money can't buy happiness, yet they insist their followers give them many strips of paper.

Even more bizarre is the magical electronic creation and storage of these colored strips. We have transcended simple control of pieces of paper and ascended into a God-like, mystical realm wherein one or two of the great "pieces of paper priests" say, "Let there be more colored strips!" And, without anything tangible, there are suddenly billions of imaginary strips deposited in the Federal Reserve, or the Treasury. Everyone cheers and is pleased that the Gods have bestowed more strips on the people. Everyone runs out and makes a sacrifice to the Gods by purchasing a new car, or a computer, or a refrigerator.

In closing I would say, what I've discovered is that these strips of paper seem to be most significant in their absence. The saddest people I've ever seen, and the happiest people I've ever seen, were without pieces of colored paper.

THE GOOD AND THE BAD OF MODERN COMMUNICATION

I try not to be too influenced by other people's opinions, because we live in an age where we are bombarded with so much information, and much of it is simply so scary you sometimes don't know what's for real and what isn't. There are diseases out there I can't even pronounce, festering, horrible things that they say were possibly spawned in the butts of camels or monkeys and transferred here on the toilet seats of foreign aircraft. We discover new maladies daily that are the result of products I've been using almost eternally! Lord! What's a person to do? We have YouTube, Twitter, email, and Lord-knows how many other sources producing questionable scenarios on everything from prescription drugs to baby food. I don't know how much of what I'm seeing and hearing is true, but believing just half of it would turn Vin Diesel into a paranoid phobic.

Every time I turn around I've received an email from someone telling me one of the most common of my daily routines is going to leave me disfigured, cancerous, or mortally wounded. Thank God I've been keeping up with the Saint Jude/Saint Theresa/Saint somebody emails that require me to send them on to at least 600 people within six minutes after receipt. It's a lot of work, but I'm not taking any chances.

In the meantime I've pretty much ruled out using my microwave, or having lemon put in my water at restaurants (who knows who dropped that lemon in there — they may have had one of those monkey/camel-butt diseases). I avoid margarine, because its apparently one molecule away from being silly putty, and I never touch TV remotes in motel rooms, because I just know one of those monkey-butt people was using it to watch porn.

I rarely shake hands anymore, because, let's face it, how many times have you seen people you know picking their noses – yeah. And I rarely use any toilet but my own because the African Killer Spider or an angry Brown Recluse may be lurking under the rim, just waiting to leap onto the more delicate areas of my undercarriage – one bite from them and you'll wish you had monkey-butt disease. I'm talking about valuable appendages getting all funky and just falling off.

I used to inadvertently check the coin return on phone booths – not anymore. Who knows who stuck their finger in that last, and who knows where they stuck that finger before they were looking for a coin? Maybe they owned a camel. Maybe they really liked that camel…

I never lick envelopes any more after reading the email about tropical bird poop being used in the glue of the sealing edge, and I never drink colas anymore, after seeing the video on what they do to battery acid.

There is so much of this stuff going around I just hate to pass on "warnings," but there is something I feel I should let the people of our area know about – because it's the time of year for ticks, and those nasty little creatures cause so much trouble.

If someone comes to your door and says they are with the County and they're checking for ticks regarding the possibly of contagious diseases, and they ask you to take off your clothes and dance around with your arms up, DON'T DO IT – IT'S A SCAM. They just want to see you naked!

I wish I'd found out about this last week – I feel so stupid...

WISDOM

Man has to grow to acquire wisdom – on an individual and on a collective basis. It always begins with knowledge found, then knowledge shared, and there are always those who seem to lead the pack in bringing wisdom to the forefront. Unfortunately, history tells us that much of the time the pack is reluctant to follow, if not outright belligerent about concepts outside their comfort zone. Many of those wise men, ahead of their time, who brought us wisdom, were branded as heretics, madmen, and fools. The world is flat, creatures don't evolve, the planets of the solar system circle the earth. Sometimes wisdom is a humbling pie, best eaten silently. And it takes courage to be a wise madman, because so many of us find it safer and easier to be wrong with our friends, than sage and alone.

Although real wisdom is a single shining light, it's often imitated by other shiny mobiles like cleverness, wit, or ego. The problem is genuine wisdom gets muddled by opinion nowadays and we have to wade through the trough of pseudo intellectuality to sift out the few real gems. Intelligence by itself is not wisdom, because intellect alone can still be the victim of greed and other baser passions. There were many brilliant people who continued to purchase shares from Bernie Madoff well after there were questions being raised.

Wisdom is what's distilled from experience and intelligence, then blended in equal parts with common sense and discipline. These are the foundations of wisdom. You can't get it in a bottle, you can't posses it by a simple Google, you can't order it on Ebay, and you can't absorb it in a Sunday sermon. It's a process, sometimes painful, sometimes insightful, sometimes elevating and entertaining, and oftentimes humbling, and it is not always related to age.

You get it by observing nature, and human nature, by taking advice, by exercising humility, by being receptive to new ideas, by remembering what you're learned, and by exercising patience. It's nondenominational, totally non-discriminating, and bereft of judgment, but it is not free.

Wisdom is one of the great principles each of us should seek during our brief visit on this ball of dirt and water because it allows us vision and provides us most of all, with a sense of perspective. Here's hoping that more of us will be blessed with the desire to ferret out and apply this elusive but rewarding element, because it is also the bedrock on which a nation thrives and grows.

Let me lighten this essay by leaving you with a quote by the writer/philosopher Elbert Hubbard:

"Every man is a damn fool for at least five minutes every day; wisdom consists in not exceeding the limit."

ONE MOMENT IN TIME

I like to believe each of us has a purpose as we come into this life, but we are born with free will and as a consequence of that free will, the onus of accomplishment and achievement is our responsibility. Greatness is not thrust upon you – it's achieved. Compassion and kindness are elements of our being we can discover or fail to discover, and environment is not always a deciding factor.

Yet, conversely, I still believe in destiny – that some of us are given, from the beginning, the possibility of the extraordinary. In this tragic and triumphant tapestry that is this world, we come upon moments that define us and oftentimes define or recalibrate our existence and the existence of those around us. Sometimes this can be as powerfully simple as one moment in time.

We've all read about Captain Chesley Sullenburger and the "Miracle on the Hudson" where this one courageously cool pilot ditched a US Airways plane with all engines out and saved the lives of over a hundred people, but there are myriad smaller stories like this that take place daily around the world – the waitress who saves a choking child with a Heimlich maneuver, the lifeguard who saves a drowning person, the taxicab driver who applies first aid to a crash victim and preserves their life, or the soldier who risks life and limb and rescues a fellow comrade. Each incident carries the incandescence of a miracle and those who were part of it will ponder on the remarkable sense of timing and luck involved with that happening for the rest of their lives. But maybe it wasn't luck at all. It could be that spirit delivered fate to their doorstep, and they took the delivery.

Maybe, just maybe, this dynamic, mercurial element we call destiny plays a part at moments like these. Could it be that the heroes of those spectacular incidents were born into this world for that single happening? That above and beyond all else, that was their moment, their purpose, this time? Maybe one person on Captain Sullenberger's plane was to have a son, and that son would find the final cure for all cancers. Perhaps the child the waitress saved was destined to write the greatest American novel, or the man the soldier preserved would become the most influential spiritual leader of the century. I know this is conjecture, but no one can deny that this is a complex, interconnected world, and with all our advancements in communication, more than ever before we all have the potential to influence the world. Albert Einstein once said, "Coincidence is God's way of remaining anonymous." When we all look back on our lives it's not difficult to find some of those remarkable coincidences.

I will leave you with a quote from one of America's contemporary icons, Steve Jobs:

"*Again, you can't connect the dots looking forward; you can only connect them looking backwards. So you have to trust the dots will somehow connect in your future. You have to trust in something – your gut, destiny, life, karma, or whatever you believe in. This approach has never let me down, and it has made all the difference in my life.*"

MEMORY...

I've discovered, regretfully, that this "getting old" thing comes with a price – nothing works like it used to. You can't see as well as you used to, you can't hear as well, and everything takes a little longer to get done. I've got a handful of parts I'd just like to trade in for new ones, but the big thing that I hear from so many of my friends is this memory issue. Young folks won't identify with this but I know a whole bunch of older people out there are going to nod their heads and smile with an acerbic understanding.

Memory is a really unique element. It's not totally necessary for most daily functions – I mean, you can play golf or tennis, or watch movies, or go fishing, and most of the time memory doesn't have too much to do with things, but try to remember where you put your car keys, or what you did with the grocery list, or why you just walked into the bedroom.

As you get older memory gets evilly selective – you can remember the names of your favorite girlfriends and the cars you owned and the experiences you had 35 years ago but you can't remember what you had for breakfast yesterday. You can remember the bad times and the good times four decades ago, but suddenly the telephone number to the bank you use is missing a couple of digits.

I love the quote by the writer Austin O'Malley, "Memory is a crazy woman that hoards colored rags and throws away food." You have to think about that for a moment.

I've begun to fall into the above categories a little more than

I'm comfortable with, so I went to the local health food store and bought a supplement designed to improve memory. I used it for a month and thought I was showing some improvement so I went back to the store to buy another bottle, but when I got there I couldn't remember the name of the product.

I've decided to print a test that I found on the Internet – to help others define how well the old gray matter is working. Now relax, clear your mind, and begin.

1. What do you put in a toaster?

Answer: 'bread.' If you said 'toast,' give up now and do something else.

2. Say 'silk' five times. Now spell 'silk.' Now, what do cows drink?

Answer: Cows drink water. If you said 'milk,' don't attempt the next question.

3. If a red house is made from red bricks and a blue house is made from blue bricks and a pink house is made from pink bricks, what is a greenhouse made from?

Answer: Greenhouses are made from glass. If you said 'green bricks,' why are you still reading these?

4. It's 40 years ago, and a plane is flying at 20,000 feet over Germany (If you will recall, Germany at the time was politically divided into West Germany and East Germany). During the flight, the engines fail and the plane fatally crashes smack in the middle of "no man's land," between East Germany and West Germany. Where would you bury the survivors? In East Germany, West Germany, or no man's land?

Answer: You don't bury survivors. If you came to any other conclusion, you need some of my memory pills. If I could just remember the name of them...

I'll leave you a quote that offers some hope for those of you who failed the test.

"The advantage of a bad memory is that one enjoys several times the same good things for the first time."

— Friedrich Nietzsche

A BEAR, A DOG, AND A SHOTGUN

I love the country life. But you can't live in a rural setting for long without having problems of one sort or another with animals – wild and domesticated. It goes with the territory. The following story really emphasizes this point.

A friend of mine called to tell me of a recent experience. He'd been having difficulties with a large, male bear that had become too comfortable with humans and possessed a nasty disposition. The animal had begun to wreak havoc on his place, tearing up food storage bins and getting into his chicken coop. One day, he came home to find the bear on the roof of his house – it had evidently crawled up there after a couple of chickens and wasn't willing or ready to come down.

Not sure what to do, my friend, Jim, called a neighbor who had some experience with bears. Wilbur, the neighbor, showed up with a sturdy, 10-foot pole, a large, heavy net, a shotgun, and a ferocious-looking Pit Bull.

"I'm gonna go up there and knock the bear off the roof with the pole," Wilbur said. "This here dog has been specially trained. When the bear hits the ground the dog will dash in and grab him by his privates, immobilizing him while I throw the net on the critter."

Just before Wilbur started up the ladder to the roof, he handed Jim the shotgun.

"What's this for?" said my friend.

The old fellow spit some chewing tobacco juice out the side of his mouth and looked at Jim. "If I fall off first, shoot the dog."

A CHILD IS BORN

Some good friends of mine recently welcomed their first child into this world, and I have appreciated, at a distance, this remarkable experience. They chose the time frame for this new soul to enter their lives, willingly acknowledging and accepting the challenges of parenthood in advance. They asked God to bless them with the stewardship of new life, and He did.

I would be remiss not to admit that the challenges of raising a child today are many, but as any father or mother knows, they fade into obscurity when you hold that tiny person in your arms and those eyes look up at you. Suddenly your whole perspective on life changes – levels of compassion you never knew existed bubble up like an artesian well – a giddiness and a weakness of the knees can be extracted with little more than a drooly grin. And Lord, the warrior/protector spirit in you rises to the surface like the call of the Valkyries – nothing is more precious, and there is no sacrifice you wouldn't make for the diminutive soul in your arms.

To my friends, and to all new parents I would say: You are at the wellspring of a life, and much of the future of this human being is dependent on you. In caring for and directing this new soul you must choose a medium between the analytical and intuitive. Nothing is set in stone. There is no single set of rules that will satisfy all situations, for you are dealing with human nature. He or she will learn more from being shown than being told. Show them, teach them, but never force them, for the branch too harshly pruned can wilt *and warp.*

Take those values you cherish that your parents have given you and pass them along, but be wise enough and strong enough to lay aside those things buried in your breast that give you pause and doubt.

Most of all, love your child always. Accept that they are another human being – a fellow traveler on this sojourn. Accept their faults and their flaws. Love them through their mistakes. Always be there for them.

It is a great challenge that you have accepted and the road along the way will be rutted from time to time, but the reward is so magnificent – to love and to be loved deeply, to know that you are not alone, to feel that hand in yours as you walk this path, to know, in your heart, you helped fashion in a positive way, the great tapestry of life.

EQUALITY AND DEMOCRACY

Equality – now here is a commodity that's been demanded since the first caveman clubbed his acquaintance by the fire for taking the larger haunch of bison. And little has changed in the last 100,000 years or so. Everyone one wants it. The problem is, there's no way to determine proportion, or to measure it accurately, and even if we could, it's basically inherent in much of human nature to want to be "more equal" than the next person.

Equality is a quirky term. In reality it defies the essence of human nature, it defeats the driving forces of ego, achievement, and accomplishment. It doesn't truly exist – it can't exist (except in some sort of robotic, Orwellian world). When you add equality to society, culture, or government, you get a continuous game of musical chairs – everyone in constant competition for more equality.

The problem with the form of democracy into which we have evolved, is that we are now demanding that it represent an equality of conditions, not just equality of opportunity. Once you start guaranteeing conditions, someone is always going to be unhappy, because you can never give some people enough to satisfy what they think they deserve.

The consensus (by Western nations) is that democracy/equality would achieve peace throughout the world. I'm more inclined to think a benign but firm dictatorship combined with a democratic form of commerce might work. People are most happy when they have definitive structure and some freedom – like children, we need to know we are free to move laterally, but that our hands will be slapped if we step out of line. This provides a sense of security, knowing there are boundaries, and that there is punishment for failure to conform to the rules of society. This is one of the basic reasons America is faltering – there are few serious punishments for breaking the rules anymore.

Equality can be a key to liberty, or it can be the hammer that crushes social equanimity. It tells us on one hand that we have no superiors, yet it's painfully apparent that every time we have a shift in social, ethnic, or religious presence anywhere in the world, we create whole new strata of superiors and inferiors.

In America we have to get past the concept that, in order to treat some strata of people equally, we must treat them differently – equal is just what it means, anything beyond that takes us right back to someone being more special than someone else. Real equality is much like utopia – it sounds great, looks good on paper, but given human nature, it's an immensely difficult proposition. Equality is a constant work in progress with a continual struggle at revision. Unfortunately, inevitably, one group just gets tired of giving what they have to others, or the others get tired of not getting as much as they think they should have. Basically that's why no true democracy has lasted more than a few hundred years.

Nonetheless, equality is a wonderful concept – something to be strived for, always kept in the mind's eye, always viewed on the horizon, like Venus just before sunrise, providing direction and a sense of purpose. We may never truly find equality, but our efforts to do so will make us a more gallant, compassionate species, and there's nothing wrong with that.

HUMILITY

Humility has a number of faces, a variety of images or conditions. It can be cast upon you by circumstance, and you can despise each moment of it, or it can come to you in an epiphany and you can carry it proudly as an integral part of your being, or you can wear it around your neck falsely like an adornment, for all to see. And in truth, maybe the condition of humility is a combination of all these things.

As you rise on the scale of success, real humility seems to take on the ethereal qualities of quicksilver – it becomes more and more difficult to keep your finger on it. But a large portion of humility is derived from understanding – understanding yourself, and the conditions of your environment, and allowing gratefulness into your life. You can maintain genuine humbleness as long as you recognize your relationship with the creator – never lose sight of the fact that you are where you are for no other reason than a benign assistance from a greater place. But never mistake true humility for weakness – humility is a spiritual power that represses ego and guile and allows a person to focus clearly. The writer Rick Warren once said, "Humility is not thinking less of yourself, it's thinking of yourself less," and that really sums it up. It's the antithesis to ego. It's seeing ourselves clearly, and ultimately this allows us to see others clearly as well.

It is an absolute requirement for the artist, the novelist, the actor, and all those of the arts, because it intercepts ego and forces the person to examine what they're doing from a standpoint of imperfection, and in this case, humility becomes a tool of integrity, or vice-versa. In addition, power and pride are dangerous elements without the texturing of humility — accomplishment, appearance, intelligence, and position should all be weighed with humbleness, because the very moment you're convinced that your scat has no odor, you're in trouble.

Basically, life is a lesson in humility. Fortunately the journey offers you a chance to find it on your own. The very best you can do for yourself is seek it out and learn to wear it comfortably, like an old pair of sneakers. Failing this, life will inevitably find humility for you, and as we all know, there's hardly anything more disconcerting than a shoe that doesn't fit. And carry a little humility in your pocket at all times. You'll find that it's much more impressive when others discover your finer attributes without your assistance.

I'll leave you with a quote by the author Andrew J. Holmes:

"It is well to remember that the entire population of the universe, with one trifling exception, is composed of others."

DIGNITY

Dignity is one of the most powerful elements in the arsenal of the well-rounded soul, and sometimes when I look around these days, I fear I see too little of it. What dignity that is lost in the older generation is not so important – its time has passed, but when I look at so much of this new generation I find a vanguard that has failed to see the value in decorum and grace. This new legion of "me first" youngsters, tattooed to the nines with their hats on backwards are rising into a world that will prove to be far less kind than the one their parents knew, and that's a bad combination. I see dignity slipping away. Worse, I see it not being sought at all, and I'd love to remind them all somehow, that being a first-rate version of yourself is far more important than being a second-rate version of somebody else.

Aristotle once said, "Dignity does not consist of possessing honors but in deserving them." This new world where everyone gets a trophy, deserved or not, is failing to teach the value of personal effort, which is one of the foundations of dignity. In the company of dignity you will always find integrity and honesty, because there is no surer way to destroy an image than with a lie. In truth, dignity is a little like virginity – it's rarely taken by force, but it's often surrendered. Along that same line, dignity is about self-respect and discipline – being able to say no and being proud that you did.

But dignity has to be real – it can't be something we feign to hide weakness or ignorance, and when it's genuine it is not diminished by the indifference of others. It is also complemented by a sense of humor, for dignity without some levity is passionless and aloof. Most of the time it's an intrinsic element that either exists or fails to exist at the core of your being. Those who carry real dignity in their breast can suffer challenging times without losing who they are. Those who have no dignity founder at the onset of difficulty, seeking the easy way out, because they lack the strength that this simple element provides.

It can't be purchased or bartered. It's something the poorest soul can have and the richest individual can lack, and true dignity is never gained by position, never lost by calamity, you are who you are, you possess it or you don't. You can't necessarily impart it but you can teach it by example, so parents teach your children well. Give them the gift of dignity.

CLASS AND CLASSES

In America, the diversity of people and the challenges of our economy have left us with distinct classes, and while there are those who would argue the merits of being in the upper echelons of America's classes, the truth is, your position in the economic hierarchy doesn't necessarily determine the class of person that you are.

Money doesn't buy you class, it doesn't buy you friends, and it doesn't buy you character. I love the quote by newspaper columnist Doug Robarchek, which says: "Money is related to class only in the minds of people who have too much of the former, too little of the latter, or none of either." This is not to say that good breeding is not a foundation for quality people, it's just that it's not the only foundation. I've spent time with "the well bred" and some of them are wonderful and down to earth, but oftentimes in the upper echelons there is a sleek undercurrent of inherent distain for those not of that stratum. Conversation contains a graceful minuet that practices the avoidance of real discussion, swiftly moving from topic to topic, tasting the meal but never swallowing it. But in all fairness, the lack of reception a butcher might get at an upper class social event might well be kinder than the reception a lost socialite might receive in the pits of the inner city. It's all about displaying class and character, not pretending you have it.

Class is really all about a confidence that comes when you've challenged life and got the better of it a few times, but it still has to be melded with a sense of compassion and a well-checked ego. Most significantly, class is about self-discipline. It's really a consistent display of integrity.

We sometimes associate class with knowing three quarters of the words in a thesaurus or unequivocally knowing which of the three forks to use with each course at a five-star restaurant, but that's not class, that's knowledge. You can train a monkey to pick up the right fork. You can't train a monkey to show character in times of peril, to be selfless, to be kind when there's no percentage in it, or to exercise pride without haughtiness. Those are the elements of class.

The decision we have to arrive at when we deal with class and classes, is that morality, compassion, and character are not the inherent possessions of any particular echelon, that that they are qualities to be ferreted out and exercised by all of us, regardless of the size of our homes or the cars that we drive. To be considerate, loving, and contemplative individuals should always be our goal, and that there is no more benefit in being blindly driven to achieve at all costs than there is to be overwhelmed, indifferent, and lackadaisical about success. If you want to possess something, possess conscience, integrity, and courage, and they will unequivocally lead you to class.

THE UNWELCOME GUEST...

The other day I ran into Rodge, my crazy buddy from Mt. Ida, and as usual, he had a story to tell me. Rodge lives in a 60-foot mobile home just off Highway 27. It's not a bad place, except that it's decorated in early bachelor. Cast-off clothes, unwashed dishes, and an assortment of beer cans are usually an accepted part of the ambience; nothing a good woman and a good cleaning couldn't fix. My buddy occasionally experiences both, though neither seem to last long enough to change that old hippie.

Rodge's latest problem dealt with an unwanted guest – a rat. It seems this giant rat (Rodge's terminology) had decided to homestead in the walls of his trailer. Now, I don't know if you've ever experienced this, but a rodent in the walls of your home can be a really disconcerting thing. It oftentimes doesn't matter how fastidious you are, they just seem to choose you, and they can be hell to get rid of.

Late at night Rodge would be having a bite to eat while watching television, and he would hear that soft patter of feet across ceiling beams, a whisper of scratching, and the rasping of tiny claws on wallboard and insulation, as the creature gathered up the ingredients essential for a comfortable little nest. He tried traps; he caught the neighbor's cat, a squirrel, and a gecko lizard, but no rat. The little fellow was clever.

The rat would scratch inside the wall and my buddy would bang on the outside and yell at him. Terrible things, he called that rat — could have burned the ears off a sailor, but the furry little guy seemed unaffected and went right on building his nest.

Now, Rodge is not known for his patience or his decorum. Gradually it began to gnaw at him — the damned rodent was outsmarting him. It was eating his house for God's sake, like it was a gingerbread cottage in some demented fairy tale! It all came to a head one night: a sordid story of whiskey, vengeance and a twelve-gauge shotgun.

Rodge had been hunting earlier that day. Having capped off the event with a six-pack, he was sitting on the couch, working on his third Jack and water (very little water), cleaning his shotgun, when the scratching began. Staring at the wall, he folded up his bore rod and put away the cleaning rags. "Dirty little $#@#$#," he muttered as he threw down the last of his drink and poured another — straight. As the scratching grew in intensity, he was sure that he could hear a squeaky, little voice laughing at him from behind the paneling. He took another swallow. The voice and the scratching continued, growing louder. He began loading the gun, four rounds of number-eight shot, one in the chamber. He focused his bloodshot eyes as best he could on the area where the rasping, taunting sounds seemed to emanate, and the barrel of the gun came around.

The cannon-like report of the weapon inside the room took even Rodge by surprise. Unfortunately, his guess as to the rodent's location was a few inches off, for suddenly, out of the smoking, jagged hole in the wall came a terrified Harry the Rat. It flew out of the hole and landed on the coffee table in front of my besotted friend. Disoriented and frightened, it bounded straight ahead onto Rodge's chest. My buddy let out *a shriek and struggled to rise, knocking over the couch as he and the rat went head over heels behind it. In the interim, the shotgun discharged again, vaporizing the small chandelier on the ceiling and instantly installing a ten-inch skylight. Harry the Rat bounced off my buddy's forehead and headed down the hallway toward the bedrooms. Rodge was quick to recover, even as toasted as he was. He was a veteran; he'd been in combat before. He scrambled for his weapon and got off two rounds as the rat squealed and dashed down the corridor. The whiskey, however, didn't improve his aim. His first shot mortally wounded the air handler for the central air system. The second round went through the bathroom wall and disintegrated the top half of the commode. Harry the Rat made it to the bedroom.*

The next day, in the process of cleanup (and $900.00 worth of repairs), Rodge found specks of blood in the hallway, but no sign of Harry anywhere. The scratching had ceased, and my friend began to savor his hard-won victory. He figured it was over, and it was – almost.

A few days later, Rodge began to sense a slightly unpleasant odor in his bedroom. A week later the area smelled like a men's room in a Guatemalan prison. Rodge looked everywhere; he even pulled the paneling off a couple of walls. No Harry. One cold morning, he took his heavy army fatigue jacket out of the closet. Putting it on and walking outside, he noticed there seemed to be a particularly disgusting stench about him. He smelled his armpits, shrugged. The neighbor's coon dogs had suddenly taken to following and yipping at him. The cold wind whipped across his face. He shivered and stuck his hands in his pockets...

The little fellow must have had a great sense of humor, for in his last moments he had crawled into his nemesis' favorite coat. It must have been a sight, seeing Rodge jerk his hand out of his pocket, rip that jacket off, then have to fight the coon dogs for it. I'd have to say the last laugh went to Harry.

COURAGE

I have always been fascinated by courage. It's the mercurial commodity in the human species – steadfast in some, devoid in others, and it seems to appear and disappear with the rest of us. It's the essence of great novels, ancient and modern history, and it's one of the gifts, if we are honest, that we most wish spirit would bestow upon us.

The truth is, fear and courage are estranged relatives. Fear is never a welcome visitor, but without it, courage would never be necessary, and what a shame that would be, because courage is one of the great expanders of the human condition. It's the mother of confidence and pride, the forger of spirit and resolution, and it's the impetus that allows us to challenge ourselves time and again. Master mariners are not made from tranquil seas. It takes a sense of dauntlessness to cast off from the familiar to begin with, but as any real adventurer knows, where there is movement, there is life.

Some individuals are genetically disposed in such a fashion as to not experience overwhelming fear. I have actually known a few people like that, and I remember marveling at the time (when I was unquestionably concerned about our immediate future) how they faced danger with such aplomb. Most of us are not so lucky. Most of us have to dig down inside and find that which allows us to go forward even when we're terrified. But ultimately that's what courage is all about – it's not the absence of fear, but the continual forward motion regardless of it. This is best epitomized by the science fiction writer, Frank Herbert, who wrote: "I will face my fear. I will permit it to pass over me and through me. And when it has past, I will turn the inner eye to see its path. Where the fear has gone there will be nothing. Only I will remain."

When I sit quietly every once in a while and run scenes from the projector that is my life, I realize that all my bravery and my cravenness, my achievements and my failures have all been poured together into one colander and sifted down to this old amalgam that is me. Like all of us, there is much I would change if I could.

If I had a young son, I would tell him he should never be afraid to set sail. I would tell him that in his life there is no doubt that from time to time he will fail, he will be afraid, he will be less than honest, he will question his course and the powers that put him where he is, and he will hurt someone he loves. But I would also tell him that the truest courage is perseverance — to never lose sight of the better person you want to be. We face challenges to our courage and our integrity every day, and we are ultimately measured by how we dealt with the small confrontations as well as the large ones — they are all a culmination of who we are. Pray courage graces you when you need it, but pray that it is a sword left mostly in its sheath.

MIRACLES

Miracles are a lot like magic. First off, to be sure it actually happened, you need to have been there, because this kind of endeavor has a tendency to grow exponentially through the number of lips from which it has passed. Secondly, everyone's version of miracles can be different. I'm reminded of the quote by author Arthur C. Clark, who said, "Any sufficiently advanced technology is indistinguishable from magic." Primitive people who view advanced science are convinced they've witnessed magic, a miracle, or both.

I'm not saying that miracles don't exist – that is, by definition, extraordinary experiences that cannot be easily explained, which generally serve some good purpose. I have personally experienced the above definition so I'm not being a critic, but let's face it, the concept of miracles is just a little bit overused nowadays. Almost as much as the term "awesome."

We spend too much time absorbed in and impressed by showmanship miracles, which may not be miracles at all – the faces of dead prophets appearing on pumpkins or tortillas, religious statues apparently crying, and people claiming to be captured in spiritual rapture and talking to God (rather than listening to Him). To me, a really good miracle is one that I'm not charged ten bucks to see. Real miracles shouldn't be the focal point of bidding wars on Ebay.

Let me tell you what I think about miracles. I have watched a small, brittle, speckled eggshell crack open and seen a tiny, mottled sparrow crawl haltingly into this life – that's a miracle. I have seen courage rise in the eyes of a common man and watched him sacrifice himself to save those around him, and that's a miracle. I have fought monster storms at sea that, for no logical reason, didn't kill me. I have been face to face with sharks, blood from a recent kill still flowing through their gills and staining the water. I have crashed airplanes, faced men with weapons intent on killing me, and been diagnosed with a deadly cancer, but somehow I'm still here to relate these stories, and you can't tell me there isn't a miracle or two in that bag. So forgive me if I'm not so impressed with the supposed face of Jesus on a tortilla.

The truth is, miracles are all around us. They manifest themselves every day. Nature is a perpetual miracle. The sun rises and opens flowers that gradually turn into fruit, the tide unerringly performs its perennial movement that preserves and refreshes the oceans twice a day, and in the midst of violence and war love still blossoms and perseveres. Miracles are often nothing more than viewing the ordinary things in life in an extraordinary way, and suddenly regarding nature and life in an analytically spiritual fashion.

Now I know there are those who would say there are no such things as miracles – it's all just a natural process, but again it's all in how you view it. To me, the natural process is a miracle in itself. It's amazing to me how easily this new, secular society will gleefully accept the latest bottle of pills from Big Pharma, promising miraculous health for this and that (and these work about half the time), but the concept of having any sort of spiritual faith clearly offends them.

I will leave you with a quote from Albert Einstein: **"There are only two ways to live your life. One is as though nothing is a miracle. The other is as though everything is a miracle."**

POWER...

Power – almost all of us want some of it. Some of us want a lot of it, and a few of us want it all. It's one of the primary elements that have driven man (and woman) to succeed, to rise above their station, and to reach for unattainable things. But the desire of it has also been directly responsible for the better part of the mayhem, chaos, and suffering mankind has seen.

Power is elemental quicksilver, given to some, wrested from others, constantly floating, swirling this way then the next, nearly impossible to hold onto for any great length of time, constantly changing partners in the dance that incorporates individuals, families, businesses, governments, and nations. Much like its younger sister, money, it is never still, always in demand, and represents the ultimate threat to your existence while providing the ultimate succor – constantly challenging the character and testing the tenacity of those who can't live without it. Abraham Lincoln once said, "Nearly all men can stand adversity, but if you want to test an man's character, give him power," and history has proven what an accurate statement that is.

The sullen, older brother of power is control – never content, threatened by or uninterested in any thought that isn't directly procured or dispensed by him. Control is more grounded in baser emotions. It's a close friend of iniquity and immorality, but it's a worrier – always concerned that its plan might slip away, always having to connive and conspire. It's a very wearing, tiring enterprise, control – not for the faint of heart. Always be suspect of any individual, organization, *government, or religion that requires extreme control.*

Power manifests itself in two versions — that which comes from threat and intimidation, and that which is derived from love. If you threaten and intimidate someone long enough you either break them, or drive them to hate you, making this form of power finite. Just ask Nero, Mussolini, or Kaddafi. But the power of love can be absolute and everlasting. It's always your choice.

In that same vein, conscience is one of the great levelers of power. It has the ability to produce insight to the tunnel vision that often accompanies this element. But it doesn't always work, because power and control are so blinding, and ultimate power, which we have seen in the Genghis Khans, the Caesars, and the Hitlers, is so seductive that the only vision is theirs. We live in a time when ultimate power has returned to popularity, and the best that we can do is pray for conscience.

I will leave you with a quote by Martin Luther King Jr.:

"Our scientific power has outrun our spiritual power. We have guided missiles and misguided men."

FATE, KARMA, AND DESTINY...

A friend and I were talking about the ramifications of fate the other day – it's a simple word with a number of complex definitions. It can represent empowerment in the accomplishments of your life, or it can represent an excuse for the lack of those accomplishments. Personally, I believe the application of fate can only take you so far, then it's up to you. Sometimes I think people accept their "fate" because they're too weak to carve out their own destiny.

Entwined in fate is a stoic commodity called karma. Karma is not really a religious ideology – it's a statement of fact – more of a moral compass that transcends faith and dogma. It doesn't really matter what religious philosophy to which you adhere, the one truism that seems consistent with most ideologies is, "As you sow, so shall you reap." That's Karma by any other definition. Fate may be more malleable. You are given many situations in life where your fate is up to you – you make stupid choices, you pay for them, that's karma. It's pretty simple.

The problem with many orthodox believers (in a variety of faiths) is that they think their dogma can control their karma, but sin makes its own hell, and virtue its own heaven. In the end we're judged by our actions, not our words. Writer Elbert Hubbard said, "Men are not punished for their sins, but by them." That's a pretty good definition of karma.

Belief in karma should make our lives pure, strong, and serene. Only our own deeds can hinder us; only our own will can fetter us. Once we recognize this, nothing in nature or the propaganda of philosophy can enslave us – and nothing can save us but our own goodwill and integrity.

To win at the game of life, you have to work hard – you have to be honest, maintain integrity, reduce or eliminate the baser emotions of hate, greed, jealousy, and revenge. You have to hone the skills of kindness and compassion, and most importantly you have to be aware that life is a constantly changing mosaic of which you are a part – and your fate is not entirely written in stone when you're born. You are the master carpenter, and you carve the edifice that is you on a daily basis.

The great philosopher Lao Tzu once said, "Watch your thoughts, for they become words. Watch your words, for they become actions. Watch your actions, for they become habits. Watch your habits, for they become character, and watch your character, for it becomes your destiny."

When it comes to fate, karma, or destiny, I also like the simple quote by the great baseball coach, Casey Stengel, who understood that individual actions set in motion our future. He said, **"See that fella over there? He's 20 years old. In 10 years, he's got a chance to be a star. Now that fella over there, he's 20 years old, too. In 10 years he's got a chance to be 30."**

LIVING AND DYING, AND 3-D GLASSES

When we are children, time seems to drift along with inexorable sluggishness. The days drag by, it seems like summer vacation will never arrive, winter is way too long, and the time between birthdays seems forever. But as we grow older there is a direct correlation between age and the speed of time. It seems to pick up pace in our late teens, then begins to move along crisply as adults, and by the time we become "seniors" it's racing at breakneck speed.

We can try to apply the brakes, put our feet out and dig our heels into the dirt, but it does little good, the time machine is out of control, and as we watch the days turn into months, then into years, we find ourselves wishing there was a "Five and Time store" down the road. But the great problem is often not so much the passing of time, but rather how satisfied we are with what we did with our share.

Some of us drift through our lives moving inexorably from day to day with the plodding myopia of a plough mule, hardly looking left or right, hardly ever hearing the music in the distance, or listening to the voice in our heart. And you know what happens after a while? The music quits playing and the voice eventually grows quiet. The antidote to this "dying in three-quarter time," at almost any point along the journey, is putting on your 3-D glasses and finding purpose. The world hasn't quit living, you have. It's the absence of meaning that steals the joy from life. You have to actually become selfish. Stop and ask yourself, "What do I want?" It might be something as egocentric as more time fishing or golfing, or it may be as selfless as needing to help somewhere, to volunteer and live vicariously from another's joy. But whatever it is, you need to find it and do it. You need to start hearing the music again.

The consensus is that you only live once. How can anyone who actually believes that be happy with squeezing less than all the juice from the orange? The choice is always yours. You can live as if you were an antidote to exhilaration, or you can put on those 3-D glasses and see what's really out there. Canadian hockey coach Wayne Gretzky once said, "You miss 100 percent of the shots you don't take," and that pretty well sums it up.

We all end up on the other side at the end of the journey, and in the last minutes of the game, just before the bell rings, we all have to give over to faith — not blind faith, but pure faith, that allows us to accept the final score with grace, instead of kicking and screaming. I am convinced that, at that point, the one thing that will make it the easiest, is how well we've played the game. Not strictly from an ecclesiastical standpoint, but a satisfied, maybe even smug view from a distance that allows you to grin and say to yourself, "What a ride it was!"

I'll leave you with a quote by former Vice President Adlai Stevenson:

"It's not the years in your life, it's the life in your years..."

WOMEN

Yesterday I was watching my wife pampering one of our cats that wasn't feeling well, and I was reminded that women are probably God's greatest gift to this planet. Their nurturing, compassionate nature, ability to endure, and the all-encompassing power of their maternal instinct have provided succor and maintained equilibrium in our species for thousands of years.

They have struggled through a morass of social and occupational inequality in the last couple of centuries and risen above it all with character and honor, and they did it without being crudely intimidating, or violent, or playing any other social "cards" like so many special interests groups.

For the longest time, whatever women did, they had to do it twice as well while being thought of as half as good. They made it look easy, and ultimately, more than any other "underprivileged" group, they exemplified the expression, "no one can make you feel inferior without your permission."

Somehow (and I still don't know quite how it was done), they raised families and raised their image in the workplace at the same time — either one of those is a challenge for a man. They may be called the weaker sex, but I'm fairly certain that was coined by a woman to disarm some man she was preparing to overwhelm.

Let's face it, they generally get the last word in every argument. Anything a man says after that is the beginning of a new argument. When a man talks dirty to a woman, it's sexual harassment. When a woman talks dirty to a man, it's

$3.95 a minute.

But ultimately, there's nothing more fascinating than a woman — men love to fish, hunt, play chess, watch sports, and participate in dozens of other pastimes, but when it comes right down to that unalterable choice, few would trade the silky, sensuous touch of a woman for any of the above, and those who do are gay.

Women have a much greater personal arsenal than men — they can arm themselves with their weakness. A few tears can collapse a man's resolve, they can say more in a sigh or a gesture than a man can muster in a paragraph, and they can cut to the quick with just a glance. And one of the most annoying qualities they have is the continual knowledge of where things are. But they are complex — they can be upset if they're stared at hungrily, and equally upset when they're not.

Men enjoy being thought of as hunters, but are generally too lazy to practice technique. Women, on the other hand, love to hunt, and they have perfected subtlety, but would rather no one knew it. Their instinct is sharper than men's. It has been honed over the centuries in thousands of little contests between each other, whereas men have just gone out and fought wars when they disagreed. Women's lives are a history of liaisons, intuitions, intrigues, and compromises, whereas men have just gone out and fought wars.

Friedrich Wilhelm Nietzsche once said, "Women make the highs higher and the lows more frequent," and there may be some truth to that, but it hardly matters, because there is nothing on God's green Earth that can replace them.

HEROES

A lot can be determined about a society by analyzing whom they consider to be their heroes. Heroism is an intricate package. It's not all about swords, and guns, and fists. It's also about persistence and perseverance in the presence of ordeal, and on the periphery it's represented by compassion, selflessness, and sacrifice. Nonetheless it's whom we perceive as heroes that defines a culture.

When we look back in history we can easily identify the champions of each civilization before us. War, religion, and politics have always been breeding grounds for heroes, from the early mythological gods, to the times of Pharaoh in Egypt, then on to people like Moses, Alexander, Caesar, Patton, and Eisenhower in the hills and valleys of time. But as man grew more refined he also began to develop a respect and eventually a passion for those of the arts, gradually amalgamating adoration of cultural accomplishment with true heroism – in the process, redefining and diminishing the nature of actual heroics.

In muddled times like these, we need true heroes to provide a yardstick by which we can measure ourselves, but the concept of a hero is becoming harder and harder to define. They still exist in the pages of novels and occasionally in the local news, but by and large our concept of heroism has suffered considerably from cultural distortion.

We have of late juxtaposed the idea of heroism with the idea of celebrity. Because you play an instrument well or act with great talent and give a miniscule portion of your immense wealth to backwards countries somewhere, does not make you a hero. Heroes earn their status through suffering and challenge, not chartered flights and champagne dinners on their way to cast dollars at children in Timbuktu. And true heroes often endure perpetual, day-to-day, unrecognized effort, doing what they do because of who they are, not what they hope to receive, or to satisfy some warped sense of ego. We have a tendency to confuse the Mother Teresas of this world with the Princess Dianas.

Sadly, today we seem to create our heroes and heroines by popular demand. We craft them by publicity to satisfy social trends. We have a half-blind, politically correct media that picks them out for us – flighty, self-absorbed celebrities who die at their own hands are somehow contorted into remarkable, saint-like personages, and sports figures whose sole talents rest in running in a single direction while carrying or bouncing a ball, are adulated as if they were gods. Rap music gangsters are suddenly more revered than firemen or doctors, and capricious, avant-garde artists are held in more esteem than teachers or scientists. Our sense of perspective has mutated. Nobleness and character has been obscured by the feverish squeals of blind rabid fans, and the powerful propaganda of television and the motion picture industry.

The concept of heroism can be a life-long commitment, or as simple as a split-second choice or a five-minute gamble with your life, and sometimes this thing we call gallantry or valor simply, suddenly rises to the surface like cream. But wherever we find it in its purest form, we should respect it. We should never compare a soldier's courage, or a nurse's sacrifice to the fanciful hobbies of movie stars, or the glamorous professions of sports enthusiasts, but we do.

People aren't "born" heroes. They are carved from their own

hardwood through trial and tribulation, and sometimes even they don't recognize that unique quality within themselves until it rises to the surface, borne of necessity. While we can continue to admire culture, and art, and artists in all their various forms, let us never confuse them with the Winston Churchills, the Abraham Lincolns, and the Martin Luther Kings, and let us never stop searching for the hero that abides in each of us, by holding in our hearts and our minds the true, unadulterated image of what a champion really is.

COYOTES, RANCHERS, AND POINTY-HEADED PROFESSORS

Man is continually unbalancing the balance of nature, and his incessant intrusion into the natural progression of things often comes back to thwart his own designs. A good example is the ongoing war between ranchers and natural predators such as wolves and coyotes.

Let me be the first to recognize the necessity of agriculture and animal husbandry in a country with a continually burgeoning population such as ours. But let's face it, when you take away an animal's hunting grounds and eliminate most of its natural prey, you can hardly be surprised when it turns to the most likely means of survival, such as cattle, chickens, or sheep.

The farmers and ranchers, who are rightfully interested in protecting their livelihood, would just as soon eliminate the problem with the old 30.30 method. This, however, incenses the conservationists and environmentalists, and instead of having just one problem, we've got several.

Living in the technicolored age of big government, sooner or later a pointy-headed bureaucrat who lives 1,500 miles from the problem (and who wouldn't know sheep wool from wolf dung) is going to get involved, and you and I will pay for a solution that will probably serve no more purpose than a band aid on a jugular wound. Case in point:

A friend of mine recently told me a story about sheep ranchers in Eastern Wyoming who were having problems with coyotes coming out of the mountains and killing their sheep. As I said earlier, they looked for a solution in the most straightforward fashion and started shooting coyotes. That got the Sierra Club involved who argued they (the ranchers) were upsetting the delicate balance of nature. The Sierra Club teamed up with the National Forest Service. They in turn found a couple of pointy-headed professors somewhere, and, after an immense amount of money (probably enough to buy each of the coyotes in question a condo in Palm Beach), they completed a study and came up with a solution.

They decided the only humane thing to do was to trap the animals live, in cages, then transfer the males to a veterinarian, where they would be neutered, and, when sufficiently recovered, returned to their area of the wild. After miles of charts, grafts, computer printouts and eight-by-ten, color glossy photos, they concluded that the males would return to the packs, and because they would no longer be able to procreate, the coyote numbers would gradually decrease to the point of not being a threat to the ranchers.

When the plan was completed, the representatives of various governmental agencies requested a meeting with the area ranchers. At the conference that day the bureaucrats presented their 3-D PowerPoint slide show, grafts and charts and eight-by-ten pictures of coyotes with and without genitals.

When it was all over, the room was filled with a stunned, incredulous silence. Finally an old rancher in the back of the room stood up, tilted back his cowboy hat, took the matchstick out of his mouth, and quietly said, "Fellas, I don't think you understand. Them coyotes ain't screwing our sheep, they're eating them."

THE GREATEST GENERATION EVER

They were, in large part, European immigrants who brought with them the value of work ethics and made those ethics an American way of life. They were the people of The New Deal, the Civilian Construction Corps, and The Tennessee Valley Authority – they paved America's roadways and built our cities, stone on stone and brick on brick. They fought in World War II and Korea, insuring and preserving the tenets of faith, integrity, and freedom for this country with their own blood.

They are the foundation, the pith and the marrow of America's present prosperity, and they are nothing less than the greatest generation this nation has ever seen. And now, America's oldest generation is silently passing on. The travesty of it all is, not only are they being refused any significant tribute, they are being ignored, shuffled, and forgotten. Their needs – social security, military pensions and health care costs, have been put aside by a government whose priorities are built around the demands of special interest groups, many of which have given nothing to this country and many of whom are not even citizens.

In an irony befitting a George Orwell novel, those who gave their all to create the freedoms and comforts we share today are, at best, being ignored, and at worst, being preyed upon by those who have no concept of sacrifice, service, or integrity.

Age is a terrible thing, not just because it steals ability and vigor, but because it diminishes image, and image, unfortunately, is what most of us rely on to draw impression.

We see an old man, eyes pale and distant, palsied hands shakily counting his change at a Walmart check-out line, and sadly, we discount him as a human being. We don't know that he was once a young officer parachuting in behind enemy lines in Normandy, and the scars he bears under his faded shirt cost him a lung, earned him a Silver Star and a Purple Heart, and bought us the freedom we have today.

The older lady in the car in front of you takes an extraordinarily long time to pull away when the light has changed, leaving you cursing under your breath. But you don't know that she once served 16 and 18-hour shifts as a nurse in a Marine tent hospital a few miles from the 32nd parallel in Korea, and her right leg just doesn't respond as it used to — the shrapnel from a mortar having torn ligaments that never healed correctly.

As you complete your daily jog, you hardly notice the old couple sitting on the park bench, faces tilted toward the warm morning sun, still holding hands after all these years. But what history lies in the etched lines on those aged faces, and what lessons they could impart. He was an engineer who helped build the Hoover Dam, she was one of the nurses who worked with Dr. Jonas Salk, and walked with Martin Luther King in Selma, Alabama. They watched America go from horse and buggy to space travel. They not only lived through the most tumultuous and momentous times in modern history, they helped shape that history.

The debt America owes its oldest generation can never be repaid, but their service to this country, the sacrifices they made that advanced and preserved this nation for the better part of its most significant century, should at least be acknowledged. They are nothing less than the greatest *generation ever.*

"Our society must make it right and possible for old people not to fear the young or be deserted by them, for the test of civilization is the way it cares for those who came before."

— Pearl S. Buck

TRUTH...

They say truth is subjective, and certainly without question, our politicians would convey that image. I suppose it can also be convenient or inconvenient — if it's inconvenient then it oftentimes becomes subjective. And truth has a great many enemies — greed, envy, anger, prejudice, and hatred are just a few. Abraham Lincoln once said, "The great enemy of the truth is very often not the lie — deliberate, contrived, and dishonest — but the myth — persistent, persuasive, and unrealistic." We see much of this in politics today.

I'm certain that truth is the most powerful weapon in any argument. Lies are like grains of sand on a beach — they erode with time and the tide, but truth is the rock that resists the water — that measures strong in any storm. It is the undeniable bond in any relationship. It carries more weight than passion, fairness, or wealth, and in the end is more durable and more valuable than love itself. You can have a deep and abiding relationship without passion, but you cannot have one without truth.

Yet, in the greatest of contradictions, it is one of the most malleable elements — because it can be twisted, just a little, by just a few words. Politicians don't lie today, they "misspeak." And in that vein, we must all beware of the half-truth — because we can never be certain which half we've received. And sometimes we're more than willing to swallow the half that pleases us, while sipping just a little of the truth we find less savory.

We practice truth in abstract today. You see it continually

in courts of law and the halls of Congress, and I'm reminded of a statement by the German philosopher Fredrich Nietzsche, who said, "The more abstract the truth you want to teach, the more thoroughly you must seduce the senses to accept it."

Our senses are continually in a state of seduction, overwhelmed by a plethora of abstract truths and cloaked falsities from commercials, commentators, attorneys, and politicians, and any real truth is getting harder and harder to find.

The greatest challenge to truth is that we all see it with different faces. What is an undeniable truth to you is little more than guise to me. Ralph Waldo Emerson explained it best when he said, "The truth is beautiful, but so are lies…" And we must sort between the two.

We are in a most confusing time for truth. Sometimes opening your eyes doesn't seem to help. I think every once in a while you must simply take a deep breath and close your eyes to see clearly. The answer you seek is not always close at hand, but the truth is.

Let me leave you with a line from the American Poet James Russell Lowell, who said, **"Those who know the truth are not equal to those who love it…"**

Love the truth, my friends…

FUN WITH THE PHONE SOLICITOR

I spent years as a Rock and Roll musician when I was younger, then went into deep diving in the Caribbean and flying airplanes. That combination of noise and pressure over the years cost me a portion of my hearing. But the best you can do with the challenges in life is to meet them head on and occasionally try to find a little humor in the cards you've drawn.

Having learned that a lack of hearing can sometimes be confusing to all concerned, I've found some wonderful entertainment in applying that to phone solicitors.

I was watching the news the other night when the phone rang. I answered it and immediately recognized the artificially sweetened voice of a phone jackal. I smiled. The conversation went something like this: (My conversation in italics)

"Hello, my name is Darell Doopey with Acme Insurance. Could I speak to the owner of the house please?"

"Well, Mr. Poopey, I own the house but I don't think I can be of any help to you."

"No, the name's Doopey, not Poopey."

"Yeah, I can understand why you changed it — that must have been miserable as a kid."

"No, my name never was Poopey. Never. It's Doopey."

"Hey, whatever you say, Gerald. I really don't care what

you're last name is."

"No, it's Darell, not Gerald."

"Listen, buddy if you can't remember your name, how do you expect me to."

(Frustrated sigh) "Okay, okay. Let's forget about my name. I'd like to talk to you about my company, Acme Insurance."

"Listen Mr. Poopey, like I said earlier, I don't think I can do you any good. I'm not a teenager – I don't have any acne, and even if I did, I don't think I'd want insurance for it."

"No, no! I'm not selling acne insurance."

"You've got an Acne Insurance Company and you don't sell acne insurance? Well, I'd change the company's name if I were you. I think that could be construed as false advertising."

"No, no! The company's name is ACME! ACME Insurance!"

"Achmed Insurance – Achmed? Isn't that a Middle East name? Are you trying to sell me terrorist insurance? You're not a terrorist are you, Gerald? Because if you are, I'd have to ask for your phone number so I can report you to the authorities."

"No, I'm not a terrorist! I'm an insurance salesman!"

"Just so I can be certain Gerald, give me your home phone number."

"I'm, sorry, we don't give out our home phone numbers."

"Why not Gerald? You have mine. That seems a little suspicious. I'm beginning to think you probably are a terrorist.

Who was the speaker of the house in the Clinton Administration?"

"Speaker of the house? What are you talking about?"

"What was Ronald Reagan's biggest western movie?"

"Ronald Reagan's what?"

"Gerald, if can't answer simple American questions like that, I bet you're a terrorist. I have to warn you that this conversation is being taped."

"I'm a flipping insurance salesman for God's sake! I'm not a terrorist!"

"That's what they all say, Gerald."

(Deep breath) "Sir, please, I just want to offer you some life insurance."

Wife insurance? Like if my wife runs off with the plumber you pay me? That sounds interesting, Gerald. I had a wife who ran off with the plumber once.

"No, no. LIFE insurance. LIFE insurance!"

"Thanks, Gerald, but I'd rather have the wife insurance. How much is that?"

"No, for God's sake! "We don't have any freaking wife insurance!"

"Then you're back to this false advertising thing again Gerald — getting me all excited about something you don't have, then trying to sell me something else. Listen, if you can prove to me you're not a terrorist, and talk to your boss about getting me some wife insurance, then maybe..."

(click...dial tone...)

Gerald? Gerald?

Who said phone solicitors can't be fun.

THE AMAZING AMERICAN SOLDIER

There are many out there today who enjoy demonizing the American soldier and the American Intelligence community – our own media are all too quick to cry about torture and misdirected bombings, and critically editorialize from the safety of distance. Like most of us these days, I'm drawn to the television in the evenings for a view of America's latest war – in the halls of Congress and the hills of Afghanistan. Although much of it is disquieting (the punishment of human beings, ours and theirs), I watched a piece the other night that left me smiling, and reminded me what a remarkable nation we are.

There was the inevitable scene of the American infantryman giving candy to children caught in the midst of war – the G.I. was dusty and his eyes were tired, but he grinned as he passed out the treats from his pack in a small Afghan village. The children in Raggedy-Ann clothing were hesitant to come forward at first, but they did, then they scampered a quick retreat with a handful of sweetness and a smile. It's the same scenario that has collapsed barriers between cultures for almost a century and I was reminded, once again, that with all our faults, we are most unique in the history of powerful nations throughout time.

You can brutally kill our soldiers, break all the conventions of war, treat us with contempt, and we will still feed your women and children, and care for your fathers and mothers. You can begin by hating us with all your heart and we will still rebuild your country, loan you money, jump start your economy, and give you an opportunity to share what we have – freedom.

It doesn't matter whether you are for or against this war, or the last one, there is no denying that in the history of the world, never has a nation so powerful been so benign, so incredibly concerned with the concept of avoiding collateral damage, and so compassionate to the vanquished.

Our military (traditionally the more conscienceless arm of most nations) is virtually willing to sacrifice American lives to avoid civilian casualties – an unprecedented concept in the history of warfare. In the very midst of conflict our young soldiers risk their lives to bring supplies and aid to indigenous populations. We adhere to the rules of warfare so completely that we make ourselves vulnerable to subterfuge and deceit by the enemy. And yet, through it all, the American soldier is always willing to grace a tiny, outstretched hand with a candy bar.

Forgive me if I gloat, but what a magnificent nation we still remain.

TIME

Years ago I sold a particularly trying but profitable business in Fort Lauderdale and returned to the Florida Keys to live. I remember driving across one of the old weathered bridges toward my new home, taking off my watch, a rather nice watch at that, and flinging it off the bridge, out into the sea below me — the gesture exemplifying that I was no longer a victim of time. It was perhaps a foolish gesture, but it was a wonderful feeling nonetheless. I was freeing myself from the bonds of duration, or so I thought...

Time is really a relative thing — for the young there's too much of it, for the old there's not enough. Half the time we can't find a sufficient amount to please us, or we've lost it (as if it were some tangible thing we stuck it the wrong coat pocket.)

There are people doing time, wasting time, and making time. There are long-timers, short-timers, and old timers, good times and bad times. Its value constantly changes, depending on the situation. It always seems that as young people we are more than willing to trade our time for more money, but when we reach a certain age, we realize we would gladly trade money for more time.

Time is really an enigma, a paradox that we struggle to come to terms with continuously. We stand rooted in the present, which is becoming the future even while we're still trying to figure out what happened in the past. It all moves in a continuous carousel, and death may well be the only exit — or is it?

One of the most fascinating things about time, in this world of inequality, is that it is totally unprejudiced. It doesn't matter how much money you have, what color you are, or what your disposition is, you can't buy extra minutes (except on your cell phone). We all are given the same number of hours in a day with which to win, lose, or draw. Carl Sandburg once said, "Time is the coin of your life. It is the only coin you have, and only you can determine how it will be spent. Be careful lest you let other people spend it for you."

If nothing else, I have watched and experienced this lifetime and I would have to say that time drags for the impatient, races too quickly for the obsessed, and seems interminably long for those who suffer grief.

I hear so often from acquaintances that they don't have enough time to do, to accomplish, to enjoy. I would remind them that they have been given the same amount of time as Bill Gates, Michelangelo, Thomas Jefferson, Martin Luther King, and Mozart.

Those who languish through life, failing to seek their dreams and offering one excuse or another for their shortcomings, often complain bitterly of wasted time. The truth is they have not so much wasted time, but rather they have wasted themselves. People say that time changes things, but mostly I've discovered that we change things if we use our time wisely.

I'll leave you with a quote that ultimately describes time best: **"How long a minute is, depends on which side of the bathroom door you're on." – Zall's Second Law**

CHICKENS...

In a continual preparation for whatever the future may hold, I added chickens to the homestead last week. Not a lot, mind you, just five laying hens, to provide us with eggs, and perhaps an avenue of barter if things really go to hell in a hand basket.

It's been an interesting experience. After converting one of my sheds to a chicken house, adding electric for heat lamps, installing a galvanized hutch, insulation, and a roof, buying feed, hay for the floor, worm medicine, feeders, and waters, I figure if each hen produces an egg a day, somewhere around the year 2016 I will have paid off my investment. But I guess you're really not supposed to look at it like that. I'm quite sure there are many Southeast Asian families that would consider my chicken house fairly luxurious accommodations, but chickens are subtle creatures and it's hard to tell if they appreciate it.

Aside from all the effort there are some things I've come to realize. First off, there's an adjustment period for chickens and the indigenous dogs and cats on your place. The dogs think this is just marvelous new entertainment, which on the plus side, can be eaten after the pleasure of chasing. The cats aren't all that interested in entertainment, but the eating part really appeals to them. It also gives them a chance to practice their stalking skills. Fortunately I got six-month-old chickens, whose size intimidated the cats a little, and my broom and I discouraged the dogs. There were some close calls I'll admit, and I was afraid I was going to have some seriously neurotic chickens that wouldn't be able to lay eggs larger than BBs, if they laid at all. But things have quieted down and the girls are doing quite well.

Another thing I've learned is that it's easier to get chickens out of a henhouse than it is to get them in. Herding chickens is somewhere on the level of herding cats. The difference is, cats are smart and they will deliberately frustrate you just for fun. Chickens aren't necessarily that bright and their reactions are pretty much willy-nilly, so there's no way to second-guess them. Now, when the chickens are out of the pen and the cats are stalking them, and you try to get the chickens back in, you find yourself herding chickens and cats, which could pretty much frustrate the Pope.

You can't yell much in the process because it freaks out the chickens, so you find yourself hissing fowl language under your breath and throwing rocks at the cats, which scares the chickens anyway and does little more than amuse the cats.

For several days after the chickens' arrival, there were no signs of eggs anywhere, so I went into the chicken house one evening and had a talk with the girls. I told them this was a symbiotic relationship and they needed to keep up their end of the deal. It could be that the word, "symbiotic" went over their heads, because the following day there were still no eggs. So, two days later I took a rubber chicken into the henhouse and just beat the bejeezes out of it in front of them. The next day I had five eggs.

Production has been good since. The cats and the dogs and the chickens have settled down to sort of a guarded co-existence, and I've found the gentle clucking sounds that the girls make as they wander around the homestead, scratching *and pecking in contentment, adds a new dimension to our country life.*

I love it when a plan comes together.

FAITH

There are a number of powerful components in the architecture of man, such as courage, honor, and compassion, but on the periphery of these are satellite elements that provide substance to insure the integrity and endurance of these components. One of these is faith.

Faith may well be the most powerful intangible in the world. It abides in our hearts and our minds, beyond the reach of proof, just past the grasp of reason, yet it is as potent as the sword and as comforting as a mother's touch.

When we think of faith, we immediately associate it with religion, and while that's accurate, its application is much broader. It's one part unerring belief, one part passionate intuition, and one part blind acceptance, and it is relevant to every facet of life. Faith in ourselves becomes confidence and it is this confidence that surges to the surface without conscious thought during times of immediate challenge. It's the belief we have in those we love and trust. It's the mortar that holds marriages together and bonds siblings. It's the common element in winning sports teams, and successful businesses. And although I contend that faith and religion can be separate entities, when they are combined they create a nearly unstoppable force. It is this mercurial combination that has given courage to those who have changed our world, and changed how we see each other. It is the faith we possess in ourselves, in each other, in our country, and in our God that is indeed the great hope for the preservation of mankind.

Faith can be brought about through different venues. It can

be a profound spiritual conviction, or an intellectual epiphany, or a powerful emotional fathoming. Prayer, of course, is often a vehicle to it, but it can be cerebral as well. It is generally the first choice in the arsenal of the devout and the final alternative in the spiritually disconnected. But somewhere along the line, almost all of us are drawn to its allure, and remarkably enough, as sort of a byproduct, the more faith you have in all facets of your life, the less control you feel the need to exercise.

But regardless of all its positive attributes, faith is most effective when it's applied with a dash of reason. This is best exemplified in the quote by Friedrich Nietzche: "A casual stroll through the lunatic asylum shows that faith does not prove anything…"

Still, it is most often what we turn to when the road darkens. At the point where hope fades, faith steps in and takes your hand to see you through. I'll leave you with a quote by Bishop W. Ralph Ward:

"Faith is raising the sail of our little boat until it is caught up in the soft winds above and picks up speed, not from anything within itself, but from the vast resources of the universe around us."

SCHOONER AND SILO

Traveling through this lifetime, my encounters with animals have been some of my more profound experiences. Some people believe that animals (dogs, cats, horses) are just animals – that they don't possess true comprehension, or a deep understanding of love. I don't believe that's true. I think love transcends and abounds within all creatures to some degree. Let me recount one of the greatest examples I can think of.

In the fall of last year my wife was driving to town when she witnessed a tiny kitten struck by the car in front of her. The people in the car slowed down for a moment, then kept on going – to their everlasting shame. Bonnie stopped. The poor little calico had lost part of an ear, and was favoring it's hip – badly shaken and crying continuously, but it appeared to have survived the incident without serious injury. Bonnie bundled the kitten in a towel and took her home.

The long and short of it is, "Silo" healed up in a week or so (albeit a little lopsided looking without the top of one ear). But Silo, less than six or eight weeks old at the time, was a wild cat – she had been raised in the grain silos and wheat fields along the highway and life had not been good. She was aggressive and aloof. She didn't covet attention as most cats do. It was hard to get her even to sit with you for a moment or two, and she wasn't blending in well with our other cats. But at this point, the strangest thing happened – Schooner, my favorite feline and our alpha cat, took over.

Schooner was a castaway also, abandoned at only a few weeks old to fend for himself. When I got him through the

Humane Society he possessed that same crystal-like hardness, the same aloofness as Silo. Like our newcomer, in the beginning he wouldn't even look you in the eye – he was just too fierce and indifferent. But I didn't give up on him. I decided I would teach him to love. Each night, after we played a little (he would draw blood without concern if you weren't careful), I would pick him up and simply hold him firmly, caressing him, whispering gently to him – teaching him the sensation of bonding. At first he resisted, squirming away and hissing, but I persisted, and eventually, gradually, I watched a metamorphosis take place. He began, begrudgingly to accept those moments, and finally, he gave into them, and from that grim, almost wolfish little creature emerged one of my dearest companions.

We didn't know what to do with Silo – she wasn't responding to our attempts at bonding. All the other cats, with the exception of Schooner, had begun to shy away from her, because she played so viciously and lacked any sense of intimacy. One night while watching television, I observed Schooner and Silo stalking and attacking each other in the living room. Then I saw the most unique thing – I watched Schooner grab silo and pull her tightly into him. She resisted furiously and I knew she was clawing him, but he held her firmly in his embrace until she calmed slightly, then he began to caresses her with his head, and gently, lovingly lick her around her ears and face. She quickly broke loose and they set to playing again. But once again, he grabbed her and pulled her into that same firm, loving, embrace.

I simply couldn't believe it. I sat there, amazed. He was using the exact method with her as I had used with him. He was teaching her to love. But he was paying for it – I could readily see the wounds she inflicted on him. Nonetheless, he was teaching her to love. Over the next few weeks I witnessed an absolutely amazing transition. Each night the ritual would repeat itself. Schooner would finally release her, then go lick his cuts clean. The embraces began to last longer and longer and Silo's resistance gradually faded. In less than a month's time, I would find them just lying there on the carpet, holding and grooming each other. I watched an animal impart a deeply significant lesson to another animal, and turn a wild, indifferent creature into a loving member of our family. To this day they are still the closest of companions — you rarely find one without the other.

I know that not all the seeds we plant in life blossom, but when they do, it's a beautiful thing...

I am reminded again of Naturalist Henry Benston's statement:

"We need another, wiser concept of animals. In a world older than ours, they moved gifted and complete, with extensions of the senses we have lost or never attained, living by voices we shall never hear. They are not our underlings. They are other nations caught with ourselves in the net of life and time — fellow prisoners of the splendor and travail of the earth."

IF WE COULD CLICK OUR HEELS...

There's no such thing as the perfect life. It doesn't matter who you are, there are always going to be challenges, pleasures, and disappointments — and choices that represent the potential for more challenges, pleasures, and disappointments. Perhaps the best measure of our contentment could be determined by a simple exercise. If you could pick a time in your life and go back to it instantly, simply by clicking your heels, would you? Now the glitch here, is you have to stay there — no coming back to where you are.

How many of us would click our heels? How many of us would think about it wistfully, with perhaps a pensive smile, and decline?

Let's be honest, most of us would love another shot at youth with what we know now. Lord, the mistakes we could avoid, the pitfalls we could sidestep, the future we could make for ourselves. But would we?

The problem for many of us is that we have to take ourselves with us when we go, and sometimes that personality we bring along will inevitably find the same pitfalls once again, and instead of a shining new path, we might well find ourselves on just another bumpy road. A change in scenery doesn't necessarily repair a defect in character.

The second problem with clicking your heels is the wager you're making — will going back with nothing prove to be more valuable than moving forward with what you have? Because once the dice are cast... We all reminisce, and fantasize with the "What if?" clause. What if we had made a different decision on mates, jobs, moves, and timely choices? But would you really click your heels on any of those?

We're all on that eternal quest for happiness and contentment but these aspects are often confounded by the inevitably of change. Nothing stays the same and it is ultimately that quality which not only adds challenge to our lives but dimension and interest.

So, I guess what this all comes down to is a paragraph I've used before: Contentment is a work in progress. It is as much about liking yourself as it is having others like you. It's about having enough money to put a down payment on happiness, but recognizing that you have to keep paying into that nest egg with a commitment of integrity and effort to make it work. It's feeling good about the future – carrying a certainty in your breast that wonderful things are still possible, and that even the end of this life is nothing more than the beginning of another extraordinary experience.

Personally, I've had a wonderful life and there were times in that life that I would love to return to, (on some occasions more than others, just like everyone else.) But when it all comes down to it, I think I'll keep my heel-clicking shoes in the closet down the hall. I just don't think I need them.

I'll leave you with one of my favorite quotes by Charles Caleb Cotton:

"True contentment depends not on what we have, but what we think we need; a tub was big enough for Diogenes, but the world was too little for Alexander."

KILLING ME SOFTLY...

The other day a friend sent me a poignant and touching story about finding the courage to put their failing pet to sleep. Having been there more times than I care to recall, I am reminded that most always we find ourselves at that junction for no other reason than compassion. It is the love we feel for that creature and the absolute abhorrence of its suffering that brings us to that choice.

I remember so distinctly when I faced that decision with my dear friend and companion, Ra, my Rottweiler, several years ago. He had fought a good fight but he suffered with a malady that in the end, couldn't be cured. And as valiant as he was, I loved him too much to watch him suffer any longer.

That final day at the vet when Ra relaxed in my arms and I knew his pain was over, there was a part of me that expected to be assailed by feelings of guilt, but all I could find was a quiet sense of peace for my old friend and myself.

On the ride home I found myself wondering how, in the greatest of contradictions, our myopic regard for life makes us so remarkably willing to allow our fellow human beings to suffer out the agonies of terminal illnesses and age-related debilitation (to the point of becoming drooling, catatonic bed sheet dividers), yet we would never consider permitting such torture or indignity for our pets.

I refuse to become too secular here, but I can't imagine the God I know penalizing me that greatly for leaving the show somewhere before curtain if my seat had become to torturous to bear, or if I had reached a point where I could no longer *discern what was taking place on stage.*

Yes, I'm well aware of the opposing arguments – the sanctity of life, the possibilities of abuse – of perhaps putting uncle Joe to sleep for his money. But speaking strictly for myself, I find little sanctity in life without some quality accompanying it. I don't want to be kept alive like a potted plant, praying for release while the last of my wealth and my children's inheritance is sucked away like the waste in the catheter beside my bed.

To quote the verse of a friend;

"Death is not proud. Nor is it avoidable. Ushering it in too quickly is wrong, of course, but trying to hold the door shut against its relentless onslaught is foolhardy at best and cruel at worst."

IS ANYONE OUT THERE?

A friend and I were talking the other day about the vastness of the universe and the possibility of other life, somewhere out there. Today, with personal video recorders and cameras in every other cell phone, more and more photographs are showing up depicting strange, inexplicable sightings of uniquely shaped objects in the sky, and more and more people, from law enforcement officers and military personal, to aircraft pilots are coming forward and telling of sightings of what can only be described as well... unidentified flying objects with designs and performance characteristics well beyond what is commonly known today.

As scientific achievement and technological advances move forward at mind-boggling speed, we are now reaching out to our own solar system (and the universe itself) searching not only for knowledge of what has gone before, but seeking the answer to the question that has intrigued and perplexed mankind for centuries – are we alone?

For the first time in the history of modern man, our technology is allowing us to record evidence of phenomena that cannot be explained away as weather balloons or pockets of methane gas. This information, and those who are gathering it, find themselves diametrically opposed to the majority of orthodox religious beliefs, and the great struggle of science and faith has found another playing field.

The greatest argument against the concept of intelligent life beyond this planet is hard, touch it, feel it, proof. Our government has done its utmost, publicly, to maintain and promote the consensus that there are a lot of weather balloons and pockets of methane gas out there.

Have I seen or experienced an extraterrestrial phenomenon? The answer is no. But in the same breath I find it somewhat conceited and naive of human kind to believe, unequivocally, that within the millions of solar systems and the billions of planets that comprise this vast and remarkable universe, there is no other life.

The greatest argument against another intelligence somewhere, is, "If they exist, why haven't they made contact with us?" At face value that seems like a fairly good contention, but when you take a few moments to examine our species, perhaps from an "outsiders" view, I think the answer becomes apparent.

There are a few constants that have existed throughout the recorded history of this planet:

* We, as a species, regardless of nationality or culture, have been killing each other continuously and randomly since the first primitive man decided he wanted the woman his companion had. We quickly graduated into wholesale slaughter as communities led to armies.

* The interesting thing about the large majority of our mayhem is that it has been, (and in many cases, still is) motivated, approved, and sanctioned by our gods.

* We are motivated by greed, prompted by lust, driven by jealousy, and 75 percent of our integrity has a price tag.

* When we are frightened or uncertain of something, our first reaction is generally to hurt it.

* Now, as we reach for the stars, we are developing horrible new weapons that can devastate entire planets. By all rights we are technological savages.

It is not to say that this planet is without creatures of kindness and compassion, and I am encouraged by the faiths that continue to promote these qualities, but it has been 2,000 years since the birth of Christ, nearly 2,600 since the birth of Buddha, and over 1,400 since the birth of Mohammed, and as a species, our overall rate of moral and spiritual development has seen little, if any, progress.

Personally, I have no idea if there is intelligent life elsewhere. But I do know that if I were an extraterrestrial having observed this planet for a while, I would give this place a wide berth and put a sign at the edge of the atmosphere – "Do Not Stop, Do Not Feed The Animals."

FACING DEATH HEAD ON

I was headed down Highway 8 East the other day, when there, on the side of the road, I noticed a raccoon. He was dead as dirt, upside-down, legs sticking up and stiff as a board. He'd obviously been looking right when he should have been looking left. As sad as it was for me to see one of God's creatures having met his fate, I couldn't keep a small smile from the corners of my mouth, for it reminded me of my first real road trip – seems like a hundred years ago. Most of all, the sight of the raccoon was a particular and poignant reminder of the fellow I had been traveling with, loony Tony Lamar. I can hardly see a legs-up animal on the side of the road, or smell peach brandy and not think of that guy. Now, I know you must think that's a pretty strange combination, but I can explain.

Loony Tony (who came by his name honestly) and I were returning from Wichita, Kansas, where I'd just bought another giant portable BBQ machine for a catering business I owned in South Florida for a while. Tony worked for me, on and off (mostly off), for about two years. If the fish weren't biting and the dogs weren't racing, or if the weather got too cold for the beach, he'd probably show up; otherwise, it was a roll of the dice. But when he did show, he was a hard worker and good company. Tony was also an excellent cross country driver, which was why he was with me that afternoon as we traveled east on Highway 40, headed for Little Rock.

We were driving straight through to Fort Lauderdale in five-hour shifts, stopping just long enough to fuel, feed ourselves and use the restroom. It was my turn to drive, so at our last stop Tony picked himself up a pint of his favorite, Morton's Peach Brandy.

We got to laughing and telling stories, and Tony began nipping seriously at that bottle. Pretty soon it was empty and he was high as a kite, crazy as a road lizard. I was thinking maybe we should find some coffee when all of a sudden he yelled, "Stop! Stop the car!"—his hands waving wildly as he pointed at something ahead, to the side of the road, a psychedelic gleam in his eye. It was a Monday afternoon; there was little or no traffic. I slammed on the brakes and swerved off the road, screeching to a halt.

There in front of us was the biggest raccoon I'd ever seen. I mean, this son-of-a-gun must have weighed in at seventy pounds. He was as dead as last week's news, on his back, legs straight out, and rigid as a fur-covered card table. Before the truck even stopped moving, Tony was out the door, yelling something about dignity and death, headed for the animal.

Sitting in the truck, I couldn't believe what I was seeing. Loony Tony had grabbed the giant raccoon, turned him over and stood him up, facing the oncoming traffic. Tony stepped back, admiring his work, and I found myself smiling, then laughing. Suddenly we were both laughing our fool heads off, and finally I understood. What was a painful last grimace had been turned into a defiant snarl as the raccoon proudly faced his nemeses — man and the automobile. He had been given a modicum of dignity in death, stubbornly standing there as if to say, "Come on, sucka', give me your best shot!" (And I'm quite sure someone did, not long after we left.) Nonetheless, it was still rewarding to see Rocky Raccoon staring onward as we drove away, a fairly empty pint of peach brandy at his side.

We were feeling so good, I let Tony buy another bottle of Morton's best, and we stood up animals for the next 200 miles. Why, we managed a little dignity for three armadillos, two 'possums, two raccoons, and a Chihuahua before we cleared Louisiana.

I guess the point I'm trying to make here, was best expressed by Tony the next day when he had sobered up. He said most everyone he knew, including himself for the longest time, was afraid of dying. We seem to perceive it as some dark, confusing affair. Somewhere along the line he realized that if you take something less seriously, it can't frighten you—that dying should be viewed with less fear and trepidation and more a simple acceptance of what it is: the final, essential part of life.

Now, I'm not saying we should take this final communion with the Great One lightly, and I'm not saying that when Grandma kicks the bucket you should stand her up on the highway. (That would freak out the tourists, wouldn't it?) But I have often wondered, at somber funerals marked with dark clothes and hushed tones, whether the one who had just passed into that bright realm would really have wanted everyone acting that way.

I've always felt most of those departed souls would have preferred to be remembered with good wine, good times, and good cheer. For me, I think I'd like to go out with a little dignity and a little levity, like a nice coffin and a Groucho Marx mask.

Y'all watch out for those raccoons, 'hear?

PARADISE

Paradise – every religion has its version, every person longs for it, some confide that it exists only in our imaginations, some get wistful and starry eyed and swear they found it and it got away, and some would argue that one man's paradise is another man's hell.

You can, of course, get technical and say it only exists on the other side, but I think versions of it can be found on a perfect lake with a good fishing rod, on a beach at sunrise, or in the arms of a stunning blonde, and tomorrow, paradise could be right where I am at this moment. To quote Hermann Hesse; "Paradise is seldom recognized as such until it's considered from the outside."

Paradise, like a good movie, gets lots of reviews. These can range from strumming on harps, singing hymns, and praising God for eternity, to 17 virgins and all the food and wine you want. If one were to study those comparisons from a strictly pedestrian point of view, it might explain Islam's rise in popularity.

All humor aside, I'm a little concerned about places called paradise that you can't leave. Even if I go to heaven (50-50 chance, maybe) I'm sure there's going to be times that I'd like to visit some of my friends in hell.

For many, Paradise is simply another version of escapism while on earth – a place you can mentally take yourself or promise yourself, that will be full of pleasure and peace, when you haven't seen or felt pleasure or peace in a coon's age. Paradise is always more intriguing to the poor than the rich.

But oddly enough, as we get toward the very end of the journey, the gap between rich and poor and heaven narrows, as we all succumb to the blind need for a comforting confirmation of life after death.

Until you reach the other side (and are remarkably overjoyed or profoundly disappointed) you should remember that a sense of paradise is always ours for the taking in the interim. It can come sneaking in on cat's feet and surprise you, or you can recognize it occasionally as it covers you with its blanket of warmth and succor. The writer Harold Pinter captured it when he said, "When the storm is over and night falls, and the moon is out in all its glory and all you're left with is the rhythm of the sea and the waves, you know what God intended for the human race, you know what paradise is."

Speaking as a wanderer and a seeker, and a person who has touched paradise this side of heaven a few times, the problem with a small taste of nirvana is that it leaves you suffering in the elemental world and wanting nothing more than another taste.

But if you want to know where paradise is for sure, I'll tell you. It's in your heart. If you have spent your years in kindness and love, and have made good friends, and had wonderful experiences in dozens of places, then you are carrying a form of paradise with you always, and what waits on the other side will only be icing on the cake.

I'll leave you with an introspective quote by Emily Dickinson:

"Eden is that old-fashioned house that we dwell in every

day. While not suspecting our abode until we drive away."

MORTALITY AND IMMORTALITY

Everyone views their mortality in a different way. Some consider just breathing an act to be cherished – some consider living well an absolute necessity, to be cherished over just breathing. Some are so concerned about dying they fail to live. I'm of the mind that Jimmy Buffett had it right when he said he'd rather die while he's living than live while he's dead.

I don't believe mortality is something to be feared. On the contrary, its finiteness lends a poignant depth to all that we do and it provides a value to the time we have here. And in truth, the uncertainty of it all reminds us how important each day is.

We are all travelers along the road of mortality – some of us take a short journey some long, some glorious, some indifferent, but it's generally our choice. It's not so much how long you stay, but what you do while you're here, and that is really the key to immortality. The renowned clergyman Harry Emerson Fosdick once said, "God has put within our lives meanings and possibilities that quite outrun the limits of mortality," and that is so true.

Immortality is not having street signs or edifices named after you. It's really about what you left here after you left. Immortality is more about what gifts you placed in the hands and minds of others. If you passed on to others qualities that make this a better world, like integrity and honesty, and they, in turn, gave these qualities to those around them, then you have become immortal. If you teach a child to fish, or to play tennis, give them a passion for nature, or a love of the sea, they will never forget who gave them that gift, and when they pass that on very likely they will tell the new recipient where that wondrous gift came from. Generations upon generations sharing gifts from a common wellspring — that's immortality. Remember, the goal is not to live forever, but to pass on something that will.

In the process, live well — take a few chances, love as much as you can, practice compassion, and teach your children well, for in each of them lies a piece of your immortality.

Finally, when we enter the realm of religion, immortality takes on another dimension — living forever and ever — in one place... In some respects that scares me more than dying. I get bored if I'm trapped inside on a rainy afternoon. I can only hope there's a bass lake or two in heaven, and maybe a tennis court.

SPITBALL

Well, it's the time of the year again for baseball. I came back from the lake last Saturday afternoon, tired and a little sunburned. Bonnie didn't have anything planned, so I stretched out on the couch and turned on the television. There was a baseball game on.

I sat there fascinated, not with the game, but with the players. I have never in my life, seen a single group of people spit so much. They are constantly gumming great wads of God knows what – chewing gum, tobacco, finger nails...

Those people have spitting down to an art form. There's the between-the-front-teeth spitters, the out-one-side-of-the-mouth spitters (or out both sides of the mouth at once if they're really good). There's the slow-drippers-between-the-legs (when they're sitting in the dugout), the chin-dribblers (accompanied by the back-handed wipe), and the reflex spitters, who manage a little spittle every eight to ten seconds no matter what they're doing. I have to wonder what matrimonial joys these guys must be off the field. Do their wives keep spittoons strategically placed all over their million dollar homes? And a fancy little spittoon for the Mercedes?

I watched players with such copious wads of Wrigley's and Red Man's best crammed in their cheeks that they looked like chipmunks wearing ball caps. Once, the game had to be halted while the umpire performed the Heimlich maneuver on a player whose golf ball-sized wad of chaw lodged in his throat as he slid over home plate. I've come to believe that cleats might not have been designed for traction, but rather to keep the players feet off the gooey mess on the dugout floor.

I'm convinced that some of those daring slides are nothing more than players slipping on infielder spit.

After watching a few minutes of the game, it was apparent that another favorite dugout pastime is nose-picking, which is often combined with spitting. Sometimes the reflex-spitters couldn't get their fingers out of their noses quickly enough and they spit on their hands. But it didn't seem to faze them. Totally unconcerned, they just wiped the concoction on their pants.

I found that nose-picking wasn't simply limited to the dugout. Every once in a while, a devious cameraman would catch an outfielder with a finger thrust to the second knuckle in his nasal cavity, blissfully pursuing an errant booger (usually trying to spit around his wrist and watch the game at the same time). I think it's very possible baseball gloves were originally made as large as they are to discourage nose-picking.

Indiscriminate scratching is another characteristic unique to baseball. Whether in the dugout or standing on first base for all the world to see, those guys scratch like a pack of baboons. I kept waiting for them to start picking the fleas off of each other in the dugout. Aside from the scratching, phlegm-flinging and nose-picking (which incidentally, makes snacking while watching a baseball game very difficult), I was amazed at how many of America's heroes, rich beyond their dreams, looked like homeless people in uniforms. Unkempt hair, like straw from Oz's scarecrow, sprouted out from underneath caps, and scraggly, two and three-day beards earmarked many a player. They appeared like color-coordinated ruffians, with poorer hygiene than a colony of spider monkeys. And each of them is making more money that the average brain surgeon.

Having spent an evening with baseball's finest, it has given me new meaning to the terms, "scratching out a living," and "spitting image."

THE GOOD DEED CLAUSE

I was talking with a friend the other day how irrefutable the good deed clause is in the book of life. "What goes around comes around" – we've all heard the expression but I don't believe everyone truly understands how geometric that principle really is.

There are those who do good in life simply because it's an intrinsic part of them. Then there are those who go out of their way to accomplish on the positive side of the scale because it satisfies an intrinsic part in them – at the end of the day, sleep comes easy and peace can be found in all corners of their world. The truth is, doing good for others is somewhat of a Machiavellian principle. As sure as you bounce a rubber ball off a wall, a kindness thrown out is going to find its way back to you at some point. It may ping-pong through a couple souls before it comes home, but it will, simply because the principle works. Mother Teresa once said, "The only people with whom you should try to get even are those who have helped you." She understood the good deed clause.

I guess what I'm saying is, there are very few of us who escape our actions. Those who understand this concept and apply it, can't help but have their lives made richer and more complete. There's nothing religious or philosophical about it. (That's not saying adding faith to the process can't enhance the result). It's more like an irrefutable law. There is no such thing as a small act of kindness. Every act creates a ripple in the pool of life. Each time you commit a random act of generosity you add a note to the symphony of life, you complete another a link in the chain by which mankind is bound.

I don't know how many times I've given someone a dollar's worth of advice and found a hundred tucked in my pocket down the road. Or how many times I've spent an hour with someone only to be saved a half-day's work later because of them. The principle works. It's as simple as that.

Life is also an adventure in forgiving. Kindness is possible even when fondness is not. Sometimes it's simply the process of loving someone more than they deserve. Every one of us remembers a time when we got more than we deserved. Most of us look back on that instance with a sense of humility and growth. Someone was using the good deed clause and we didn't even understand it at the time, but we appreciated the results.

If you want your life to be more than what it is, you have but to apply this concept. First, reach inside yourself and find the desire to make this a better world. Then simply reach out and help someone — touch their heart if it needs healing, listen to them when they need a friend, make their day a little easier, their course a little clearer, with your hands and your words. It's like money in the bank. It's the "everyone wins" lottery of life and all you have to do to win, is to play.

So, as you begin this day, make a conscious effort to practice the good deed clause. You are a part of the great pool of life. Create a ripple...

To purchase an autographed copy of any novel by Michael Reisig, go to *michael-reisig.com*. Reisig's novels are also available in eBook format through Amazon.com and Barnesandnoble.com

The Truthmaker

Florida Keys adventurers Trace West and Zach Zapeta find their lives turned upside down when they discover a "truth device" hidden in the temple of an ancient civilization. Enthralled by the virtue (and entertainment value) of personally dispensing truth and justice with this unique tool, they take it all a step too far and find themselves drawn into a whirlwind of intrigue involving a secret international organization and a conspiracy that will shake the foundations of America.

Along the way, from Key West, into the Caribbean, across to Washington D.C., and back to America's heartland, West and Zapeta gather a wild collage of friends and enemies – from a whacked-out, one-eyed pilot and an alluring computer specialist, to a zany sociopath with a zest for flimflam, a sadistic "problem-solver" for a prominent religious sect, and the director of presidential security. **($12.95)**

The Road To Key West

The Road to Key West is an adventurous/humorous sojourn that cavorts its way through the 1970s Caribbean, from Key West and the Bahamas, to Cuba and Central America.

In August of 1971, Kansas Stamps and Will Bell set out to become nothing more than commercial divers in the Florida Keys, but adventure, or misadventure, seems to dog them at every turn. They encounter a parade of bizarre characters, from part-time pirates and heartless larcenists, to Voodoo *bokors,* a wacky Jamaican soothsayer, and a handful of drug smugglers. Adding even more flavor to this Caribbean brew is a complicated romance, a lost Spanish treasure, and a pre-antediluvian artifact created by a distant congregation who truly understood the term "pyramid power." **($12.95)**

The New Madrid Run

The New Madrid Run is a tale of desperate survival on an altered planet. In the aftermath of a global cataclysm caused by a shift in the earth's poles, a handful of survivors face the terrible elements of a changed world as they navigate a battered sailboat from the ruins of Florida into the hills of Arkansas via a huge rift in the continent (the New Madrid fault). They survive fierce storms and high seas pirates only to make landfall and discover the greatest challenge of all... **($8.95)**

The Hawks of Kamalon

Great Britain, Summer, 1944

A small squadron of British and American aircraft departs at dawn on a long-range strike into Germany, but as they cross the English Channel, the squadron vanishes.

Captain Ross Murdock and the '51 Squadron are cast into a whirlwind adventure of intrigue, treachery, and romance as they are "culled" back and forth across the universe, outwitting and outrunning the Germans, while they attempt to foil the invasion of Azra by the neighboring continent of Krete. **($7.99)**

The Old Man's Letters

Meet Jake Strider, a cantankerous country sage with a caustic wit and a ribald sense of humor.

The Old Man's Letters chronicles some of Strider's most notable correspondence to his son over almost two decades. It's a hilarious, remarkably perceptive panorama of rural life, from bizarre tales of crazy friends to poignant political and social points of view. This is a guaranteed "laugh out loud" read. **($8.95)**

Printed in Great Britain
by Amazon.co.uk, Ltd.,
Marston Gate.